Here is writing that is both humble and spiritual, as piercing as a sunbeam in a darkened room. Each of these nuggets glorifies the commonplace and points out new directions and adventures for the masses who are crowding life's road seeking light and truth.

CHARLES L. ALLEN *is pastor of the First Methodist Church of Houston, Texas, one of the nation's largest Protestant congregations. Known widely through speaking engagements, through radio and television appearances, and as a newspaper columnist, he is the author of a number of inspirational books that have enjoyed sales of over a million copies.*

Books by CHARLES L. ALLEN

- ROADS TO RADIANT LIVING
- IN QUEST OF GOD'S POWER
- GOD'S PSYCHIATRY
- WHEN THE HEART IS HUNGRY
- THE TOUCH OF THE MASTER'S HAND
- ALL THINGS ARE POSSIBLE THROUGH PRAYER
- WHEN YOU LOSE A LOVED ONE
- THE TWENTY-THIRD PSALM
- TWELVE WAYS TO SOLVE YOUR PROBLEM
- HEALING WORDS
- THE LIFE OF CHRIST
- THE LORD'S PRAYER
- PRAYER CHANGES THINGS
- THE TEN COMMANDMENTS
- THE SERMON ON THE MOUNT
- THE BEATITUDES
- LIFE MORE ABUNDANT

*for
Leila,
Charles, Jr., Franklin
and Mary Jane.*

Appreciation is expressed to
The Atlanta Journal-Constitution
for permission to use the material in this book.

Contents

The Birth of This Book 9

1. THE CENTER OF THE HURRICANE 13
2. THREE IMPORTANT STEPS 15
3. BESIDE THE STILL WATERS 18
4. WHAT'S WORRYING YOU? 20
5. STEPS TO FORGIVENESS 22

6. FORGIVE YOURSELF 25
7. LET GOD HEAL YOU 27
8. HOW TO STOP SOMETHING 33
9. HOW TO START SOMETHING 35
10. GETTING WHERE YOU WANT TO GO . . 38

11. CONTROL YOUR EMOTIONS 41
12. LEARN TO HOPE 43
13. MAKE UP YOUR MIND! 46
14. GET PEOPLE TO LIKE YOU 49
15. LEARN TO PRAY 51

16. LEARN TO BELIEVE 54
17. BELIEVE IN SOMETHING BIG 57
18. GUIDES FOR RIGHT AND WRONG 60
19. GET GOD'S GUIDANCE 62
20. NO SITUATION IS HOPELESS . . . 65

21. HELP FOR THE ACHING HEART 67
22. SEE YOUR OPPORTUNITIES IN TROAS 70
23. COUNT YOUR DREAMS, TOO 73

7

24. THINGS THAT MATTER MOST	76
25. MASTER YOUR HANDICAPS	78
26. HANDLE YOUR DISAPPOINTMENTS	81
27. WAIT FOR YOUR EASTERS	84
28. THROW AWAY YOUR WALKING STICK	87
29. THAT FEELING OF SECURITY	90
30. BE YOURSELF	93
31. GETTING ALONG WITH PEOPLE	95
32. THE LIFE INSIDE	98
33. HAVE A PLAN	100
34. SOMETHING WORTH FIGHTING FOR	103
35. A LITTLE HONEY	106
36. PATHS TO PROSPERITY	109
37. ON BEING HONEST	111
38. IT IS BETTER TO GROW OLD THAN TO SHRINK YOUNGER	114
39. AID TO YOUR MEMORY	116
40. GET ACQUAINTED WITH THE CHRISTIAN FAITH	118
41. THE INSPIRATION OF A GREATER PERSON	120
42. FAITH IS CATCHING	123
43. USE YOUR FAITH	126
44. YOU KNOW ENOUGH TO BE SAVED	129
45. LET CHRIST CHANGE YOU	132
46. MEET THE MASTER	135
47. KNEEL AT THE CROSS	137
48. HIS SEVEN WORDS ON THE CROSS	140
49. KNOW THE LIVING CHRIST	143
50. GET "ON THE WAY"	147
51. ROADS MAKE THE TRAVELING EASIER	150
52. FORGET IT!	153
53. LIFE IS GOOD	155

The Birth of This Book

ONE OF THE burning ambitions of my early life was to play baseball for The Atlanta Crackers but, just a few weeks before I finished college, I was offered the pastorate of three little country churches. I wrote my father, the Reverend J. R. Allen, himself a minister and a very wise man, and asked him what I should do. He replied that I should decide whether I wanted to be a preacher or a baseball player. At the age of nineteen, therefore, I became a pastor.

But the Lord takes care of those who trust Him, and eventually Bishop Arthur J. Moore sent me to Grace, the Methodist Church closest to the Atlanta baseball park. The bishop was giving me a wonderful chance, but he had more faith in me than I had in myself. I had lived in little country towns all my life and I knew nothing about a big city church.

Eighty years before, Grace was started as a community church among Atlanta's nicest homes. But the city had grown and business had pushed the people farther out. The church had suffered somewhat by the change.

In one of these chapters I tell about my first Saturday afternoon at the church and my own rededication.

Above all things, I had set my heart on a great Sunday-night service, but the chances for it looked a little slim to me. During the following week I visited the book stores of Atlanta and asked to see the books the people were buying most. I reasoned that if you preached on what people were most interested in, you would get a better hearing. I set out to prepare my sermons along the lines of peoples interests and needs.

I asked one minister what type of a night service city people would like best. He said, "A short service." He told me that he never held his people more than forty-five minutes and that his church was always "comfortably filled." What he meant was that there was room enough for everybody to lie down.

I planned a service to run about an hour and a half. We have simple songs that people can sing. I preach as best I can and then invite people to come and pray at the altar. We now average nearly a thousand each Sunday night, about two-thirds of whom pray at the altar. The spiritual atmosphere in this service has worked many miracles in human lives.

It is certainly not my preaching that is important. My sermons are very simple and ordinary. But it does make a tremendous difference when people kneel before God in simple faith, knowing that "all things are possible to him that believeth."

Later, Mr. George C. Biggers, president of *The Atlanta Journal*, gave me a chance to write a column each Sunday, for which I shall ever be grateful. Soon afterward, radio station WSB made available to me time for a talk each Sunday afternoon.

As a result of these wider opportunities, I have received many letters and have talked privately with as many as time would permit. I have wonderful opportunities to study people and to try to apply the eternal principles of God to their needs.

The messages in this book are, for the most part, my columns in the Sunday *Atlanta Journal-Constitution*, which, in turn, came out of my Sunday-night sermons at Grace Methodist Church.

Atlanta, Georgia. CHARLES L. ALLEN

*Roads to
Radiant Living*

1. The Center of the Hurricane

ONE OF THE greatest losses we Americans have suffered is the old-fashioned fireplace. A generation ago, the folks would gather around after supper, put on two or three fresh logs, and sit there basking in the warmth and watching the flames dance up and the red coals slowly turning into ashes. There was no radio, not much to read, so they would just sit there an hour or so and talk a little, but mostly just sit and think about things, slowly rocking in the old rocking-chair.

When bedtime came, it seemed the natural thing to reach up on the mantel, take down The Book, and read a chapter or two. Then it seemed right to the family to get down on their knees and thank the good Lord for all He had done and to pray that His overshadowing arm might be about them as they slept.

Naturally, a good night's sleep followed such an evening. And the next day minds were clear and serene. Out of such a life came what we call the "fireside faith."

I am not calling for the "good old days" again. I enjoy living in an automatically steam-heated house. Yet I never heard of a "radiator-side" faith, or a "warm-air register" faith. One of the fond dreams of my life is to have a little cabin not too far away with a wood fireplace where I can go occasionally and just sit, think and watch the fire, and slowly rock. I would be a better man for it.

A man came to see me and said he needed help. I

asked him to tell me his story, and he talked for about twenty minutes without my saying a word. He was all mixed up in his home life, his personal life, and now his business was about ruined.

I asked, "What do you plan to do?" He thought a few moments and then told me the steps he planned to take. I said, "That sounds like a good procedure to me. I do not believe I can suggest anything else." Then he got up and said, "You have solved my problems for me." He thanked me heartily and left.

But I had not solved anything. I had not even said anything. The solutions were entirely his. After he left I sat thinking about this business of personal problems, which all of us have in one form or another.

I remembered when a hurricane was headed toward Florida. The Army Air Corps wanted to make some studies of hurricanes and sent a plane out to meet this one. When they got to it, they flew straight into the center. It was the first time any person had ever flown into the center of a hurricane. When they got inside, they found not rain or high winds, but a perfect calm. It was so calm and peaceful that they flew around inside for some time. Later, one of those boys said that he would never be afraid of a hurricane again—if he could only get to the center of it.

And I realized that what my visitor had done was simply to sit down calmly and in an ordered way think and talk himself into the very center of the hurricane of his own life. Then, in such a frame of mind, he could see the way out, and it gave him confidence and peace.

I had not done anything for him except be quiet and listen. Any number of his friends could have done the same thing for him. Any number of our friends can do it for us. We can even do it by ourselves.

Thinking about this man who was troubled, and about

the old fireside, makes me realize again what so many of us need most. It is a "place of quiet rest—near to the heart of God." If we can just get at the center of these things that upset us so we would find a calm there and, in that calmness, begin to see the way out.

Three very great truths from the supreme Book of Truth come to my mind—"They that wait upon the Lord shall renew their strength" (Isaiah 40:30); "Thou wilt keep him in perfect peace, whose mind is stayed on thee" (Isaiah 26:3); and "In all thy ways acknowledge him, and he shall direct thy paths" (Proverbs 3:6). There we have it. Get quiet and wait. Saturate your mind with thoughts about the good Lord and you will begin to see the way out. Strength, peace, and guidance will be ours. What more could we want?

2. Three Important Steps

QUITE FREQUENTLY I do not get home until after my little children have gone to bed, but I always go into their room and look at them. They are sound asleep, perfectly relaxed, and there is peace on their faces. I ask myself why it is that the people I have seen that day cannot have the peace that I see in my children.

All of us had that childlike peace at one time. But, as we grow older, our lives become more complicated. We think of making a living and we worry about our debts, or our jobs, or taking care of ourselves in our old age. We bother about the world situation. We get crossed up with other people, we become upset thinking of our health, we want to improve our social position.

We do things that are wrong and we fail to do things that are right, and our consciences hurt. We develop little civil wars inside ourselves. We cannot relax, so we get tense and nervous. Because we do not have peace of mind and peace of soul, we get sick and life becomes an unhappy burden.

A physician whom I admire very much asked me recently to come into his office with him certain hours every week and talk with some of his patients. He said that in many of his cases his treatment was ineffective because the patients were so agitated and upset. He said that before their bodies could be healed, they needed to find mental peace.

If we could only find again that perfect peace that we had as little children, life would take on new joys and thrills that many have even forgotten exists. So I want to point out three steps that will help anyone to find mental peace.

First, GET THE POISONS OUT OF YOUR MIND. You may have had a pain in your side. You went to the doctor and he found that your appendix was bad and that before you could be well it would have to be taken out. Or maybe it was an abscessed tooth that your dentist discovered that was poisoning your system. The abscess had to be healed before you could regain your health.

More often it is not a physical poison that is hurting you. Is there something on your conscience? Have you done some wrong? Are you angry with anybody? The step to take is genuine repentance through faith. The Divine Surgeon can reach into your mind with His own scalpel and tenderly remove the thing that is poisoning your soul. God still forgives.

Note carefully these words: "Oh what peace we often forfeit, O what needless pain we bear, all because we do not carry everything to God in prayer."

Second, FILL YOUR MIND WITH THE RIGHT THINGS. One of the greatest songs ever written is, "Count your many blessings, name them one by one." I suppose it is not great music but it is good sense. Instead of concentrating on your problems, just sit down quietly and begin to name your blessings. It seems a simple thing to do, but the results you will obtain will amaze you.

Think of something beautiful. Think, for example, of two dozen red roses. Picture them scattered out on a table. Then, in your imagination, begin to pick them up one by one and arrange them in a vase. It takes some practice, but God gave us our imaginations to use and something beautiful in your mind helps to bring peace.

A fine aid to mental peace is to think about a person whom you admire, one who is good and strong. All of us know some people whose very presence gives us strength and courage. As we think about them we are inspired and helped.

The prophet Isaiah gave us the formula for mental peace: "Thou wilt keep him in perfect peace, whose mind is stayed on thee" (26:3).

Of course, most of us can more easily fill our minds with God by thinking of Christ. "He that hath seen me hath seen the Father," Jesus said John (14:9). That is why I so often suggest that the reading of the four Gospels helps people so much.

Third, ACCEPT YOUR RESPONSIBILITIES AND OBLIGATIONS. As we start doing the things we feel we should do, it makes us feel good inside.

Silas Marner was a bitter, unhappy miser until he lost

his gold and found a little golden-haired girl. As he began to love and live for her, he found happiness and peace. You will never find peace so long as you think merely of yourself and your own interests. "He that loseth his life for my sake shall find it" (Matthew 10:39).

These are three steps to mental peace.

3. Beside the Still Waters

IF YOU COULD look at this man who came to see me, you would think that he never had had a worry in his life. Big, strong, manly, successful in business, he owns a nice home, has a lovely family, and is highly respected by his friends. I was surprised when he told me he was sick, and I suggested that he see his physician.

But he had already been, and, after a number of tests and examinations, his physician had told him he was in perfect physical health. But when he kept insisting that something was wrong with him, the physician had suggested that he have a talk with me.

I asked him his trouble; it was that he could not sleep at night. He told me he had not had a full night's sleep in six months.

I named a current book on how to sleep that is having a good sale; he had already read the book, and had not been helped. I asked about his bad habits, but he seemed to have a lot fewer than I have, so I dropped that approach. I asked about his conscience, but he assured me he had done nothing that was disturbing him.

I told him that he was not alone in his problems, that every night six and a half million Americans took a "sleeping tablet," but he said he had taken so many that even those did not help him any more.

I thought of giving him one of my sermons to read at night—I notice a good many people have gone to sleep while I was preaching them. I did suggest that he go to church every Sunday night—that will help a lot.

We continued talking, and finally he said, "I have everything a man should want in life, but I am just plain scared and I do not know why I am scared."

I took a sheet of paper and wrote across the top of it these words: "HE LEADETH ME BESIDE THE STILL WATERS." I handed him the sheet of paper and told him to put it in his pocket and before he went to bed that night to write down under the quotation everything he thought it meant and whatever related thoughts it brought to mind. Then he was to put the paper in his dresser drawer. The following night he was to take out what he had written, read it over, and add whatever additional thoughts had come to him. He was to keep that up every night for a week and then come back to see me.

I wanted to saturate his mind completely with that one thought. I know that it is utterly impossible to keep fear and thoughts of "still waters" in a mind at the same time. Any good fisherman can testify to that. That is the reason that fishing is such a great medicine for so many people.

There is no nerve medicine on this earth to be compared with still waters; when we create those clear, cool, still waters on the screen of our imagination, it is wonderworking. As Longfellow put it, "Sit in revery, and watch the changing color of the waves that break upon the idle seashore of the mind."

Well, I wish I could say that this man came back the

next week refreshed, relaxed, and at perfect peace. But, to tell the truth, he did not come back at all. He felt he was too big and important for such a simple little exercise. He wanted me to tell him something complicated and mysterious, and when I told him such a seemingly simple thing to do, he was disappointed.

I would like to point out to him that greater scholars than he can ever be have studied that familiar phrase, and that no one has yet taken all the meaning out of it. And I would also like him to know that men become great because a great thought possesses their minds.

Alexander Hamilton once said, "Men give me credit for some genius. All the genius I have lies in this: When I have a subject in hand, I study it profoundly. Day and night it is before me. My mind becomes pervaded with it. Then the effort which I have made is what people are pleased to call the fruit of genius. It is the fruit of labor and thought."

"He leadeth me beside the still waters." Sweet, peaceful sleep comes easy to any person whose mind is saturated with that one thought.

Of course, no medicine ever works for those who will not take it, and one must take the entire prescription. Those first three words are more important than the "still waters."

4. What's Worrying You?

BY HER VOICE over the telephone I judged her to be a very cultured woman about sixty years old. She was very careful not to tell me her name or anything about herself that would have enabled me to guess her identity. But obviously she was very upset and needed help.

She told me that her children think of her as a very good woman but that actually there was something on her conscience that had worried her for many years and now she could no longer stand it. She said it was something she had done as a young woman. More than anything else, she said that she wanted peace—peace of heart—but that with this thing on her conscience she could not have it. She called me to ask what she could do about it.

Ordinarily, when people talk to me about past wrongs, I never let them tell me too much. In the first place, I have heard about everything that one might be guilty of; and, in the second place, often people will reveal things when they are upset that later on they will regret having revealed. But in this instance, because I did not know the person, I felt it might be helpful to know exactly what she had done that was worrying her. So I asked for the details and she told me that as a young lady she worked in a store. One day she took a little change out of the cash register, meaning later to replace it. A few days later she took some more, and then for about a year she continued to take small amounts of money.

It seemed harmless at the time. It was a big store and could afford to lose the money, especially because she felt that they were not paying her as much as she thought she was worth. But this is just another example of the fact that you cannot justify a wrong, even to your own conscience.

This dear lady got my sympathy. Imagine her carrying such a burden on her conscience for probably forty years! The nights she had tried to sleep and could not because of that burden! The times she missed all the beauty of this wonderful world about her because her mind was darkened by something ugly. The times her children got on her nerves and she scolded them unjustly! It wasn't nerves, for the children were normal; it was the burden of a guilty conscience she was carrying.

A life, perhaps fifty per cent wrecked, when it would have been so easy to straighten it all out and make peace within her own heart.

Well, I was glad to be able to tell her what to do and I hope that she did it and will have peace of mind and peace of heart during her last days. First, she must make such restitution as she can. It will be all right to send the store anonymously what money she can afford. Then, just for the asking, she can have the pardon of God. And, finally, she must be willing to pardon herself. To get her own pardon will be the hardest for her, and I suggested some ways to go about it.

But, over and over, I keep thinking, how terrible it is to torture ourselves and spoil our lives over past wrongs that could so easily be righted and put out of our lives forever.

5. Steps to Forgiveness

I STUCK A splinter in my finger. It was not a big splinter but I took careful pains to get it out. I knew there was the possibility of that splinter setting up an infection. And, if let alone, that infection could go up my arm and through my body, and even could kill me.

Now, the human mind is a lot like the body. The mind can be wounded. Things can get into the mind that will set up an infection that can destroy a life.

Sorrow is a wound. But sorrow is a clean wound and, unless something gets into sorrow like self-pity, bitterness, etc., the mind wounded by sorrow will heal.

Sin is a wound. But sin is an unclean wound and, unless it is removed from the mind, it will never heal. Instead, it will go out over your nervous system and make you jumpy and jittery. It will go to your heart and accelerate its action. It will go to your stomach and upset your digestion. Sin is the wrecker of more lives than any other disease.

When I do something that violates my standards of right and wrong, I have put an unclean thing into my mind. It may not be a very big thing and, like the splinter in my finger, it may seem not to amount to much, yet even a very small wrong can set up an infection within my mind.

A very prominent physician said to me only recently that many of his patients did not need to see him. They needed to see a minister who could help them cleanse their conscience.

Instead of sleeping pills, a lot of people need an old-fashioned period of repentance. Instead of a new drug, a lot of us need an experience of forgiveness. We need to get right with God and with our own conscience.

A person cannot do wrong and get by with it. You cannot stick a splinter in your finger and just ignore it. It must be removed. The same is true of a wrong in the mind.

Time and again, I have prescribed to people the Fifty-first Psalm. It is David's prayer of repentance.

David had done wrong. He had reached the point where he could not continue to live with himself.

In that prayer he prays, "Have mercy upon me, O God." Justice is not enough. Only through God's mercy is forgiveness possible.

"I acknowledge my transgressions." He does not tell God he is no worse than somebody else. He pleads no mitigating circumstances. He frankly admits he has done wrong.

"Wash me, and I shall be whiter than snow." He has faith that forgiveness is possible. He believes that no person is hopeless in the hands of the Great Physician.

"Create within me a clean heart." He wants to be guilty no more. He is willing to change his way of living.

"Restore unto me the joy of thy salvation." He recognizes that happiness is possible only to one in a right relationship with God.

"Then will I teach transgressors thy ways." If he is healed he promises not to be ashamed of the physician. He will tell others.

Those were the steps that David took after he had committed terrible sins, even murder. And they lead him to the place where, later, he could say, "The Lord is my shepherd; I shall not want."

It worked for David. I have seen those very same steps work wonders in the lives of many, many people.

Some time ago Mary Pickford wrote a little book, the title of which was, "Why Not Try God?" Well, why not? We have tried nearly everything else, and a lot of us are still miserable and unhappy.

I said that to a person not long ago and his reply was, "I have so completely neglected God that now I am ashamed to face Him."

I asked him whether he would be ashamed to face his physician if he were sick? Or whether he would be ashamed to face his mechanic if his car broke down?

Then why be ashamed to face Him who loves us completely and who can always heal?

Indeed, why not try God?

6. Forgive Yourself

I TALKED WITH a man who was in such a nervous state he could not do his work. His business was going down, his home life was unhappy, he was avoiding his friends, and had started drinking heavily.

We found that his trouble stemmed from a terrible thing he had done some years before. He had tried to forget it, but the thought of it was increasingly in his mind. He would think about it during the day and even dream about it at night. His mind had become almost completely obsessed by this one memory.

It was something that required no restitution, and now there was nothing he could do about it. But he was deeply repentant and seemed to me to meet every condition of forgiveness. I read and explained to him the Fifty-first Psalm, which is David's prayer of repentance. Then we got on our knees and prayed for God's forgiveness.

I feel absolutely sure that God completely forgave that man that day, that the Father wiped the slate clean and remembered the man's sin against him no more. I told him that and he believed it. I felt he would be all right.

But the next week he came back, no better than he had been. I said to him, "God has done something for you that you are unwilling to do for yourself. You asked God to forgive you and He did, but you have not forgiven yourself." He agreed, but insisted he could not get it out of his mind.

I reminded him that in the New Testament Jesus tells us to become as little children. I asked him if he remembered ever falling down and hurting himself when he was a little boy. Of course, he remembered.

"When that happened," I asked, "what did you do?" He did what all of us have done. He went crying to his mother and she would kiss the bruised places and, in some mysterious manner, the pain would go away and he would feel well again. He smiled as he thought about it.

Then I suggested that now he be like that little boy. I told him that he had bruised his heart, his soul, his conscience, that it hurt terribly, but that the great Father would kiss the pain away if only he would believe. I told him to believe in God just as he used to believe in his mother. Not to be big and important, but to have the simple faith of a little boy.

Again we knelt together, and I prayed, "Father, here is one of thy children who is hurt. Now he has come to you as he used to go to his mother. He is kneeling at your knee. Take his pain away—right now." We got up, and he said, "For the first time I feel it is gone." And I can report that today, after some months, he is a radiant, happy man.

There are many people who are living a condemned life because they never learned to accept the forgiveness of God, that is, to forgive themselves. Many people carry on their minds an accumulation of past mistakes, failures, and sins. It becomes a burden that no person can bear. It produces terrific mental strain, nervousness, fear, and worry.

Walt Whitman said: "I think I could turn and live with animals, they are so placid and self-contained. . . . They do not lie awake in the dark and weep for their sins." It is true that animals do not feel guilt. But it is also true that animals do not write poetry, as did Walt Whitman.

In man there is something good and fine. He is made so

that he can "lie awake and weep over his sins." Take that out of man and he would be no more than an animal. But a sense of guilt can turn a strong man into an invalid. It can produce all sorts of functional disorders. It can wreck one's mind.

One can be so overwhelmed with a sense of guilt that one of three things happens. He will be turned into an animal without conscience or hope. Or life will become unbearable, as it did for Judas. Or one will accept and be loosed by an experience of forgiveness—God's forgiveness, and then his own.

Time and again I have read to myself and to others a poem that Ernest Rogers wrote, which he called "Another Chance." One of the verses goes:

> But down on my trembling knees I fall,
> Though others may look askance,
> To say a prayer to the Lord of All,
> The God of another chance.

No matter what you have done, remember, "If my people, which are called by my name, shall humble themselves, and pray, and seek my face, and turn from their wicked ways; then will I hear from heaven, and will forgive their sin, and will heal their land" (2 Chronicles 7:14).

7. *Let God Heal You*

ABOUT TWO-THIRDS OF the recorded ministry of Jesus was healing the sick. Truly He was the "Great Physician." Not only did Jesus heal, He gave His followers the authority to heal and commanded them to do it. (See Luke 10:9.)

As we study the work of the early Christians, we find that healing was one of their normal activities. Peter healed many, as did Paul, Philip, and the others. James says: "And the prayer of faith shall save the sick" (James 5:15). I can find no record or evidence that God has ever taken away from people of faith the power to heal. It can be used today just as it was used in the Early Church.

However, some people feel one must choose between Divine healing and the healing through our physicians, hospitals and marvelous medicines. But there is no conflict between the science of medicine and surgery and the science of faith and prayer. They work together like wings of the same bird.

Luke was a physician when he became a Christian. He certainly believed in Divine healing and says more about it than any of the other Gospel writers. Yet he did not throw away his medicines after he became a Christian. He continued to practice the rest of his life.

A man suffering from diabetes came to see me some time ago. He said, "If I believed in healing through prayer and faith, does that mean I should not take insulin?" I said to him that God made insulin and that the physician is also a minister of God. And that God expects us to use the means at our disposal.

In fact, I refuse to pray for any who are sick who are not under the care of a physician. Our men of medicine and surgery, our nurses and our hospitals, are doing the work of Christ, and to deny ourselves their ministry is to act very unwisely. I frequently tell people to go to their physician for diagnosis and such treatment as he prescribes.

However, I know that the science of prayer and faith is also powerful and effective in healing the sick. A doctor was showing me not long ago a new X-ray machine he has. It is a complicated mechanism and wonderful things can be done with it. The physician can turn electrical power through that machine and send X-rays into diseased tissue, often with miraculous results. I believe in the X-ray and I know it works.

And I also know that when a man kneels to pray, he is a much more mysterious and complicated mechanism than a machine made of glass and metal called X-ray. And when the power of God begins to flow through the life of a consecrated man or woman strange and mighty things can and very often do happen.

Prayer and faith quiet the mind and allow the curative powers of the body to work more effectively. Also, prayer and faith strengthen the will to get well and give hope and courage. But Divine healing is much greater than mere psychology. It is the power of God.

The most appealing example of Divine healing that I know is found in Mark 9:14-29. A father had brought his son, who was suffering with epilepsy, to Jesus.

Jesus first asks the father, "How long is it ago since this came to him?" The Lord is asking the father to start at the very beginning and tell Him about it. This is a method used today in psychoanalysis, which Freud made famous.

A lady once came to Dr. Freud suffering from what seemed to be an incurable disease. She wanted to tell him her troubles, but he insisted he could not help her. However, she wanted to pay his fee and tell him, anyway. At least, it would help her to tell her troubles to somebody.

She came regularly each week, and after a few weeks he discovered that she was actually getting well. Often the miracle is accomplished through telling someone the entire story. In my own ministry I have seen it happen again and again.

And it is good to talk to someone. The greatest thing is to "carry everything to God in prayer." Our God is a great God and He has time to hear you. I know it helps tremendously.

Then Jesus said, "If thou canst believe, all things are possible to him that believeth." You must come to God in faith. I have forgotten most of the Latin I ever learned, but I do remember that the great Virgil said, "For they conquer who believe they can." If you are sick, believe that you will get well and it is probable that you will.

Now comes the most appealing part of this story: "The father said with tears, 'Lord, I believe; help thou mine unbelief.'" Those tears are precious. He did not come to God on flippant, irreverent feet. He was deeply sincere and in earnest.

And, as you read between the lines, you hear him saying, "Lord, I do believe, but I must be honest and tell you that my faith is not perfect and complete. I want you to help my unbelief."

The father loved that boy so much. Since he was a little fellow he had been having those spells. They could never leave him alone, for fear he might fall in the fire. He could not play with other boys, and the father and mother would pray so hard, but it did not seem to help.

Doubtless they had carried him to the church and the ministers and others had prayed, but neither did that help. Of course, the father had carried him to the physicians and bought every new medicine that came along, but still the boy got no better. So many times the father had hoped, only to be disappointed every time. It was natural that his faith was not perfect and complete.

None of us has perfect health. In the mind of every person there is a little doubt. And especially when one has been disappointed so often. But this father did not let his disappointments and doubts keep him from seeking the help of Jesus. He is honest and humble, and he comes with what belief he has, admitting his unbelief.

Remember, Jesus said, "If ye have faith," not a full and perfect faith, but "as a grain of mustard seed," that is, a little faith but one that is growing and developing. Then "nothing shall be impossible unto you" (Matthew 17:20).

And Jesus healed the boy!

I believe tremendously in the power of faith to heal the human body, both mentally and physically. *Reader's Digest* (January, 1940) had an article, "A Patient Goes to Dr. Cushing." The patient felt that he was going mad, and finally got an appointment with the eminent brain specialist.

After examination, the doctor said, "You came here thinking I would send you to the madhouse. Forget it: you're all right." The patient said, "I believed him. He was sure, and he made me know he was sure. . . . I went into his presence a tottering wreck; I left him confident and happy." He was healed by his faith in Dr. Cushing. The Great Physician is far more able to heal.

A woman in Atlanta had completely lost her sense of smell for some years. One Sunday night she prayed at the altar at Grace Church, completely committed her life to God, and asked Him to heal her.

The next morning, as she was cooking breakfast, she was suddenly aware of the aroma of bacon. She could not believe it, and called in a man working in the yard and asked him if he could smell it. She told us the man thought she was crazy to get so excited over the smell of bacon cooking, but it was really something to rejoice over for one who had not been able to smell anything for so long. Her sense of smell now is perfectly normal.

Faith in God creates a hopeful, optimistic mind. Many are familiar with a demonstration used by Coué. He would place a twenty-foot plank twelve inches wide on the ground and any person could walk it. But if the same plank were raised to the height of a cathedral, almost no one would even dare try to walk it.

You see, if the plank is on the ground any person can create the mental picture of achieving. But when the plank is high in the air the mind creates the picture of falling. So when one is sick. If you believe in the power of God to heal, your mind creates the picture of getting well. But if you feel your case is hopeless, then you probably never will get well.

Also, faith is a unifying power within a life. Frequently I have had people say to me, "I have gone to pieces," and they have. We commonly use the expression, "Pull yourself together." But it is hard, sometimes impossible, to pull oneself together without help. Faith in God is exactly the help one needs.

Just as a house divided against itself cannot stand, neither can a divided life. And often the first place where inner conflicts show up are in one's physical health. Man is filled with conflicting emotions and impulses, and he can never be well and happy unless over them all there is one guiding and reigning king.

> Within my earthly temple there's a crowd;
> There's one of us that's humble, one that's proud;
> There's one who's broken-hearted for his sins,
> There's one who unrepentant sits and grins;
> There's one who loves his neighbor as himself,
> And one who cares for naught but fame and pelf.
> From such perplexing care I would be free,
> If I could once determine which is Me!
>
> (Author unknown).

I do not understand the power of God to heal, any

more than one understands the power of radium to heal; but I do know that when one sincerely commits his life to God's will and believes, very often miracles of healing are accomplished.

And the power of God is not only present to heal, but to meet every other need of your life. "My God shall supply all your need" (Philippians 4:19).

8. How To Stop Something

HOW TO STOP something you *need* to stop! Nearly everybody is interested in that because nearly every person has something that needs to be stopped. It may be a habit, such as gambling, drinking, or profanity. It may be some mental habit, such as self-pity, impure thoughts, jealousy, worry or a failure complex.

There are four simple steps which, if carefully and persistently taken, will free us of any habit of action or thinking which enslaves us:

(1) Decide exactly what it is you need to stop. And that is not always simple or easy. For example, a man told me he needed to stop being critical of other people. But the cause of his critical attitude was jealousy. Underneath his jealousy was a very real feeling of inferiority. The reason for that was the fact that he was lazy. What he needed to stop was being lazy.

There are vast numbers who need to stop drinking. But that involves a special process which Alcoholics Anonymous is using in a perfectly superb manner. But many drinkers are not alcoholics. They drink because of the crowd they associate with, or because they are trying to escape from something. Maybe it is because they have not found any satisfying outlets of expression, or maybe they are unwilling to put forth the effort that living requires and find that alcohol is a simple substitute.

(2) You must decide whether or not you really want to stop. My little boy sucks his thumb. I never have bothered him about it because I feel that the harm sucking his thumb will do is not nearly so great as what is done to the personality and nervous system of a lot of children whose parents set out to make them stop.

But one day I decided to have a talk with him about it. So I asked him why he sucked his thumb. He said, "Well, I'll tell you. I suck my thumb because I want to so good." And so long as he feels that way I think I had better let him alone about it.

One of the profoundest truths of psychology is that whatever you really want done probably will be done.

The reason that we often have difficulty in stopping something is that our minds are divided. One part of the mind says, "I ought to stop this." The other part of the mind says, "I like this, and I do not want to stop it." And that mental division squanders one's power of decision.

(3) The next step is simply to make up your mind to stop. There is a verse of Scripture that applies here: "Be strong, and quit yourselves like men" (1 Samuel 4:9). Just quit acting a baby. Don't sit around whining and whimpering, complaining and excusing. If you are going to quit, go ahead and quit.

(4) But these three steps are not enough. They would be enough if each one of us possessed a resolute, undefeatable, iron will. But we do not have that. Therefore, the big fourth step is the most important one. Say over and over

until you have planted them indelibly in your mind these words: "I can do all things through Christ which strengtheneth me" (Philippians 4:13).

The Gospel does not tell us to "try harder." What it does tell us to do is, "Believe harder." There is tremendous strength in belief in Christ.

Here is one way it works. By using your will power you say you will stop. But your imagination, which is stronger than your will power, tells you that you cannot stop. Thus you are defeated.

But when you admit your own weakness and fill your imagination with Christ, marvelous power begins to flow in to support your will. As you see Christ before the tempest and the winds and the waves become peaceful under His magic skill; as you see sick people become well under His power, lame people throw away their beds when He speaks, and captives set free by His power of deliverance, gradually you begin to realize that nothing could defeat Him, and, as you consecrate your life to Him, you come to the thrilling realization that, because you have Him, *nothing can defeat you.*

9. How To Start Something

IN THE LAST step we were thinking of "How To Stop Something You Want To Stop." But it is better to know "How To Start Something You Want To Start." Now let us consider four simple steps for starting what you want to start.

First, fix clearly in mind what it is you want to start.

Someone has well said that the world turns aside and gets out of the way of the man who knows where he is going. You can't expect to get anywhere if you do not know where you want to go.

Georgia Harkness says, "Be careful what you set your heart on, for you will surely get it." Know exactly what it is you want to start.

Second, get started. It is good to call to mind that old story of how the devil wanted to destroy the world. He called his chief assistants. First came Anger, who said, "Let me go and destroy man. I will set brother against brother. I will get men angry with each other and they will destroy themselves."

Next spoke Lust. "I will defile men's minds. I will make love disappear and men will be turned into beasts." Then Greed said, "Allow me to go and I will instill in men's hearts the most destructive of all passions. Man's own uncontrolled desires will destroy him."

The twins, Gluttony and Drunkenness, came and told how they could make men's bodies diseased and their minds besotted. Envy, Jealousy, and Hate each told how he could destroy man. Idleness claimed he could do the job.

But with none of these was the devil satisfied. Finally, his last assistant came in. This one said, "I shall talk to man persuasively in terms of all that God wants him to be. I shall tell him how fine his plans are to be honest, clean and brave. I shall encourage him in the good purposes of his life."

The devil was aghast at such talk. But the assistant continued, "However, I shall tell man there is no hurry, he can do all of those things tomorrow. I shall advise him to wait until conditions become more favorable before he starts."

The devil replied, "You are the one who shall go on earth to destroy man." It was Procrastination—just put it off a while longer.

Somebody wrote these lines:

He was going to be all a mortal should be, tomorrow;
No one should be braver or kinder than he, tomorrow.
The greatest of workers this man would have been, tomorrow.
But the fact is, he died and faded from view,
And all that he left here when living was through—
Was a mountain of things he intended to do, tomorrow.

Get started. NOW spelled backwards is WON.

Third, believe you are going to succeed. One of the dramatic sports events of all time was when Babe Ruth pointed to the fence in a World Series game in Chicago and then drove the ball over it for a home run.

After the game a reporter said to Babe Ruth, "Suppose you had missed that final strike?" A look of surprise came over Babe's face and he said, "Why, I never thought of that."

A lot of people start with doubts and thoughts of failure in their minds and they fail almost every time. Nothing will dissipate your power faster than to think failure. But those who fill their minds with resolute faith, who think positively instead of negatively, go on to victory.

It is simply amazing what one can do if he will keep believing and keep trying. Often, however, that is not easy. The human mind will resist struggle. It will want to give up in surrender. It will seek the dead peace of hopelessness. To keep believing positively is difficult, but it is the pathway to power and victory.

Fourth, rely on a power greater than yourself. When I lived at Blue Ridge, Georgia, I used to go often to the big power house below the dam. There I would watch those giant dynamos as they brought power out of the universe that would run factories, pull buses, and light up cities.

And remember, the God who created electricity did not

forget to create a power for man that would pull him over the steep hills of life. When, with humility of spirit, we go into partnership with God, a new and a thrilling power comes surging in.

Plant deeply and persistently in your thinking these words, "I can do all things through Christ which strengtheneth me" (Philippians 4:13).

10. Getting Where You Want To Go

THERE ARE A lot of people who are unhappy in their present circumstances and would like a different life. Many go through life unsatisfied and never accomplish the things they want most to do. So I would like to point out how any of us might get where we want to go.

First, SET DEFINITE GOALS. Some time ago I wanted to buy for one of my sons a picture to hang in his room. I wanted it to be one that would inspire and help him whenever he looked at it. We finally selected Burnand's "Go Ye Into All The World."

It is a simple charcoal drawing of Christ and the young man John. As Christ is telling John to go into the world, He seems to be looking at the entire horizon. But John's eyes are more definitely fixed on something specific. I have told my son that he might teach, preach, farm or do any of a number of things, but that he would have to decide on some definite goal.

I preach constantly the probability that one will become what he pictures in his mind, and that if one thinks about going to nowhere in particular he probably will end up there. Suppose someone asked you, "Can you tell me the way?" Immediately you would ask, "The way where?"

If you are unsatisfied with your present life, stop and decide exactly what it would take to make you happy. Fix it clearly and firmly in your mind.

Second, START WITH WHAT YOU HAVE. It is a fact that most of us have more resources and abilities than we ever use.

By my desk is an electric fan. In the summer it renders me a fine service. I used the same fan last year and probably will use it many more years. But suppose I took hold of the blades and held them while the switch was on. Soon the motor would burn up. That fan must either burn the power that comes into it or the power will burn the fan.

So in a human life. You must either use the energies you have or those very energies will do you positive harm. Instead of using their power, a lot of people are letting their power burn them.

Third, TRUST IN THE HELP OF GOD. A man who had not been getting along very well came to see me. He had found it hard to make a living and, because of that, the home life was not very pleasant. We talked at some length about what he would rather do, and he decided he would rather be a mechanic.

In fact, he had tried to get a job in a garage but because he was inexperienced, no one would hire him. I was convinced of his mechanical abilities and told him that if he would consecrate his life to God, live as God wanted him to live, and have faith, God would help him. We knelt in prayer together and I was impressed with his dedication.

The very next day another man came to see me. I asked him what his work was, and he told me he was a mechanic. I told him about the other man and asked if he would help him. He was glad to do it, and the first man now has a good job doing what he wants to do and has a fine future ahead. When I told him that God would help him, I had no idea that the very next day a man would come to see me who could help him. But I will always believe that God sent that man.

When I came to Atlanta as the pastor of Grace Church, I admit I was, in the words of the popular song, "bewitched, bothered and bewildered." I had never been pastor in a big downtown church and knew little about it. On Saturday afternoon before I was to preach my first sermons I came to the church to look around.

The building seemed so big that I doubted that there were enough people in Atlanta to fill it. Frankly, I was as scared as I have ever been. The thing I wanted most was a great Sunday-night service, but that Saturday afternoon I was quite shaky about it. In fact, I would have been glad to swap for a church in some little town.

But I knelt at the altar and that day made a new dedication of my life. I promised God all I had and asked for His help. The first Sunday night we had chairs in the aisles and we have needed them every Sunday night since. And when I say that God will help you I am not preaching, I am testifying. He will help you to get the things you want and you can count on it.

One of my favorite texts is: "If ye have faith as a grain of mustard seed . . . nothing shall be impossible unto you" (Matthew 17:20).

11. Control Your Emotions

To GET AHEAD in life and to be happy, you must learn to CONTROL YOUR EMOTIONS. I want to give four simple suggestions that will work wonders for all who try them.

First, STUDY YOURSELF and determine your weak spots. Achilles had a vulnerable heel, and nearly every person has some particular weakness that upsets him. For example, I know people who can endure prolonged physical suffering but will go to pieces at the slightest criticism.

One of my vulnerable characteristics is impatience. I have friends who can fish all day in one spot and have a perfectly marvelous time whether they catch anything or not. I cannot do that. I actually believe I was born in a hurry, so that when things go slowly I get irritated.

I have recognized that weakness and have made a lot of progress. One afternoon I was driving out of downtown Atlanta about 5:30 o'colck in the afternoon. The traffic was heavy and slow, and I had to creep along. I was beginning to get upset, and then I caught myself.

I thought about how long it would take me to drive from where I was to my home if there were no traffic at all. I decided it would take ten minutes. Then I looked at my watch and decided to see how long it would take in that heavy traffic. Then I just relaxed, turned on the radio, and settled down.

It took me exactly sixteen minutes to get home. Just six minutes more. I was thoroughly ashamed of myself. There

I was about to get upset over six minutes. I decided that my time is not that valuable.

Study yourself. What are the things that irritate and upset you? I dare say that in most instances they are simply not worth bothering about at all. So study to strengthen yourself where you are emotionally weak.

Second, STUDY PEOPLE. The study of people is the most interesting study in the world, so, instead of letting some person upset you, study them objectively.

For example, suppose a store clerk is rude to you. Instead of getting angry and making a fool of yourself, start asking yourself why the clerk is rude. Perhaps a previous customer had upset him, and he was taking it out on you. A member of his family may be very sick, and he is worried. Perhaps he has a toothache, or is worried over a debt and doesn't know how he can pay it. If you knew all the facts, you probably would feel sorry for him instead of being angry with him.

Instead of letting people upset you, get interested in them and you will learn a lot and maintain your own self-control at the same time.

Third, STUDY THE PRICE YOU PAY FOR GETTING UPSET. You may have to pay a doctor and a medical bill. You may even have to go to a hospital. A physician told me recently that fully half of his patients were sick because of emotional disturbances. When you become sick you lose time from your work and cannot do a lot of things that you would do if you were well.

Or your emotional uncontrol may destroy your home. Nothing in life is more precious than the love of wife or husband. But if you keep on "flying off the handle," saying things you do not mean, pouting and nagging and acting like a spoiled brat, that love can be killed. To lose the peace and joy of your home is a mighty high price to pay.

You cannot do your work nearly so well when you lose your self-control. Thus you drive away customers, or cheat yourself out of a promotion. You are forced to swallow the bitter pill of seeing your fellows get ahead of you.

Finally, RECOGNIZE THE PRESENCE OF GOD. I used to play golf with a man who was addicted to profanity. Yet, because I was a minister, he never uttered an oath in my presence. When I was with him he controlled himself.

Now, if he fully realized that at all times and in all places he was in the presence of Almighty God he would never utter another oath.

Mrs. Fulton Oursler says that she used to count up to ten when she found herself getting upset, but that it did not help much. Then one day she noticed the first ten words of the Lord's Prayer. So now, instead of counting ten she says over and over, "Our Father which art in heaven, hallowed be thy name." When one's mind becomes saturated with those ten words their influence is magical.

The prophet Isaiah said, "In quietness and in confidence shall be your strength" (30:15). To become strong, learn to control your emotions.

12. Learn To Hope

ONE MORNING I ran across this saying: "Life is full of glad surprises for those who hope." It stuck in my mind and I found myself repeating it over and over. At noon that day I spoke to a group of business men and, as I often do, I spoke too long, making me late for another appointment.

I rushed out to catch a bus back to my study, but just as I got to the stop, the bus pulled off and I missed it. I was about to get fretted when I thought of the saying, "Life is full of glad surprises for those who hope."

So, instead of fretting, I stood there on the corner, hoping. In less than two minutes a man stopped in a big Cadillac and offered me a ride.

On our way, we talked about several things, then he said to me, "You are doing a lot of things, and you need a rest." I had heard that before, however, so paid no attention.

But then he said, "I own a lovely hotel down in Daytona, Florida, and I want you and your family to go down there and stay as long as you can." Then he said the most important thing, "You will be my guests, absolutely without charge."

After I got out of his car, having graciously accepted his invitation, I just stood there thinking about it. So often we foolishly fix our minds on things we have missed in life when, instead, we ought to be looking ahead and hoping for something better to come along.

Dr. Samuel Johnson, one of the greatest minds England ever produced, once declared that to have a bright outlook on life was worth a thousand pounds a year. It pays off, even financially to think optimistically.

When I got back to my study that day, I read again Psalm 42:5: "Why art thou cast down, O my soul? and why art thou disquieted in me? hope thou in God: for I shall yet praise him for the help of his countenance."

"Hope thou in God." That is to say, when you are discouraged and disquieted, put God in the center of your thinking. Plant deep in your mind the persistent, persuasive feeling that God is on your side, and, somehow, everything will be all right.

The Psalmist says that if you will do that, there will

come a time when you will have reason for praise because of what God did for you.

Recently I have been studying again the Ten Commandments. In connection with the third one, we naturally think of profanity. But most of the swear words we use are more stupid than sinful.

To my mind, the most profane word in the English language is the word "hopeless." We say a situation is hopeless, or a person is hopeless. And that is literally a denial of God. "Hope thou in God"—with God nothing is hopeless.

One of the greatest men who ever walked this earth was Abraham. In explaining his greatness, St. Paul says in Romans 4:18, "Abraham, who against hope believed in hope." Moffatt's translation makes that clearer: "For Abraham, when hope was gone, hoped on in faith." There were times when things looked very dark for Abraham. He went out "not knowing whither he was going." But no matter what happened, he kept on hoping—looking and working for something better. And that something better did come.

One of my favorite paintings is the canvas by Watts, entitled "Hope." It is the picture of a woman sitting on the world, a world that had dealt unkindly with her. Her eyes are bandaged, indicating that she cannot see her way ahead. In her hands is a harp, all the strings of which save one are broken. Those broken strings represent her shattered expectations. But the one string left is the string of hope.

Triumphantly she strikes that last string, hope, and from it there comes a glorious melody that floats out over her world and fills her dark night with stars.

It is the painting of a great truth, the truth that if we will just strike the string of hope in faith when all else is gone, somehow our souls will be set to singing again.

I have before me a letter from a friend telling me of a

marvelous change that had come into his life. He says, "I have something else to think about, and a new hope."

Certainly it is true that "life is full of glad surprises for those who hope."

13. Make Up Your Mind

I ASKED A banker friend of mine what he considered the secret of his success. He was very modest about it and protested that he had not done very well, but it is a matter of record that he is one of the most astute bankers in the South and is considered an outstanding success by all who know him.

Not willing to claim any credit for himself, he said that what he had been able to accomplish was the result of some advice that he got from his first employer. This employer took him just after he finished college and put him in a responsible position. Then he told my friend that the secret of success was this: "WHEN YOU HAVE A DECISION TO MAKE—MAKE IT AND GO AHEAD."

The employer told him that he would make mistakes but no more by deciding quickly and definitely than if he dilly-dallied and took a month to decide. The employer further pointed out that so long as one has decision hanging over his head he is weighed down and misses further opportunities. The young man followed that advice and has done very well because of it.

That interested me, because it so happened that I had just read what Mr. J. L. Kraft, the cheese manufacturer, had replied when someone asked him to what he attributed his success. Mr. Kraft said it was his ability to make up his mind.

In counseling with many people, I have come to believe that one major cause of failure, unhappiness, and tension is inability to make a clear-cut decision. David Starr Jordan used to say, "The world turns aside to let any man pass who knows where he is going." The ability to make up your mind inspires self-confidence, it gives you inner power and it commands the respect of your fellow men.

One of the great loves of my life is baseball. To be a great hitter in baseball one does not have to get a hit every time he goes to bat. In fact, a player can fail two out of every three times and still make any baseball team in America. But to me the most disappointing sight in a game is to see a player stand with his bat on his shoulder and let the third strike be called on him. To swing and miss is not so bad, but to stand there and not do anything is terrible.

So in life. Every decision one makes does not have to be the right one; even the wisest will make mistakes. But if you ever expect to succeed, you have got to be willing to make some decisions, to take some chances and go on. To stand through life with your bat on your shoulder is to fail in the worst way.

I was talking with a man recently about joining a church in Atlanta. He said he had been thinking about doing that ever since he moved to Atlanta. Seven long years he has been here, with his bat on his shoulder, gradually being called out.

One can settle certain large problems in life with just one decision. For example, think of marriage. The reason a lot of marriages break up is that one or both parties involved have never fully and completely decided. After marriage, the thought of possible happiness with any other person should never be entertained, even for one minute.

For me, giving has never been a burden since I decided to tithe; when I am faced with some cause to which I should contribute, it is no struggle trying to decide whether or not to give. It is merely a matter of looking into my tithe account and apportioning what I can to that particular cause.

Or think of honesty. A person should decide once and for all whether or not he intends to be honest. Then the temptation ever to be dishonest or to tell a lie is never a bother. There are many questions which one can settle with just one decision.

Trust in God to help you make the right decisions. The Psalmist said, "Thou shalt guide me with thy counsel and afterward receive me to glory" (Psalm 73:24). The Psalmist believed that God's wisdom is available to people and that if we will avail ourselves of His guidance by putting our lives into His hands through consecration, He will "afterward receive us to glory," that is, He will see to it that, somehow, everything works out all right.

When he started out peddling cheese in a one-horse wagon, Mr. Kraft believed what the Psalmist said, and his business grew to the point where he now has a fleet of trucks covering America. In explaining his method, he said: "When I have a decision to make, first, I pray hard. Then I think hard, and when the time is about up and I must have the answer, I say, 'Lord, now you show me the next thing to do.' Then the first idea that comes into my mind after I have gone through that process is what I take to be the answer. I have been correct a large enough percentage of the time to persuade me that this course is sound."

A friend of mine told me that when he has a decision to make, he first prays, "Lord, I want to do the right thing, and, if you will show me what the right thing is I promise you I will do it, regardless of what the cost may be." He says he usually has very little trouble making up his mind after that. When one puts himself on the side of God and the right, he may be sure of the guidance of the wise Father.

Life is better for him who learns to make up his mind.

14. Get People To Like You

WHAT DO YOU want more than anything else in life? Someone asked a group of high school students that question and the large majority of them said they wanted to be popular. William James knew more about people than any American ever has known, and he said that one of the primary cravings of human nature was to be appreciated.

In fact, there is something radically wrong with any person who does not want to be liked by other people. People do a lot of things to try to impress other people. It is natural, and I think good, that we do want to be liked.

Occasionally someone says that Jesus Christ was not popular. Don't ever believe that. He was the most popular man of His day. In fact, that is the reason He was crucified. A group of crafty people in power plotted His death because they were afraid He would lead the people away from them.

Multitudes followed Jesus wherever He went. Little children rushed to hug Him. His list of dinner engagements reveal that he was sought by all classes. Great parties were given in His honor. And any person who sincerely follows Christ also will be popular.

However, we must remember that if we seek popularity we will never find it. It is like happiness—it always comes as a result of something else.

Also, we must remember that there is no such thing as getting everybody to like us. The best thing ever written on "How To Be Popular" is the twelfth chapter of Romans. There we find listed the things we should do. But then St. Paul adds, "If it be possible . . . live peaceably with all men." He wants you to understand that you will find some people that you cannot be popular with.

That ought not to bother us, because none of us completely likes himself. I had that brought home very forcefully to me only recently. I was preaching in a series of revival services. The local radio station recorded my sermons and rebroadcast them in the afternoon. So I would sit during the rebroadcast and listen to myself preach. I had to admit that I had heard preachers I had rather listen to. So when someone indicates he does not like my preaching I am a bit inclined to admire his judgment.

But if you really want people to like you, here are three simple steps to follow that will help. First, DO A GOOD JOB. Bobby Jones will always be one of the most popular men in the world of sports. Why? Because he did a great job in golf. We will always love Margaret Mitchell because she did something fine in literature.

Who is the most popular person in your office or business. It is usually the one who does his work conscientiously and well. Whatever your work is, do your best and people will admire you for it.

Second, LIKE OTHER PEOPLE. Someone has pointed out that "a gossip is a person who talks about others; a bore is a person who talks about himself, and a brilliant conversationalist is one who talks about you."

Dr. Hugh Black said this about Jesus: "In the company of sinners, He dreamed of saints." That is, whomever He saw, He was looking for his possibilities instead of his faults. In a world as big as this we do not need to compete with each other; there is room enough for us all.

Third, GET RADIANT INSIDE. Some philosopher once said that the thing that makes some people more attractive than others is "the lighted candle in the soul." Some people are dead inside.

Once at church I had the ushers give every person a small candle. I had placed a large candle on the altar. At the proper time we turned off the lights, and each person came forward and lit his candle by the one on the altar. And the best place to light the candle in your soul is kneeling at some altar in faith and consecration.

15. Learn To Pray

THE LIGHTS WERE burning, the janitor was running the vacuum cleaner, and the organist was playing a beautiful melody as I walked into my church one morning. Into the building some wires run, over which flows that marvelous power that gives light, that cleans up and produces harmony.

Now, the God who created electricity did not forget to create a power that will do those same things for a life. And the channel through which that power flows is what we call prayer. The disciples once said to Christ, "Lord, teach us to pray." It is the only thing they ever asked Him to teach them. They knew that, once they learned to pray, the power of God was at their disposal.

In response to that request, Christ gave them seven simple steps to follow. He needed only sixty-six words (Matthew 6:9-13), and the power is available to any who follow those steps.

(1) Start by thinking of God. Forget about your own needs and problems for the time being and saturate your mind with thoughts of God. This will silence the mind and bring relexation. Think of Him as "Our Father which art in heaven." You cannot imagine a cyclone in heaven. Heaven suggests calmness, beauty, and rest. Note the first word is "Our." You cannot pray for yourself alone.

(2) Then let your prayer begin with thanking God for what He has done for you. Think of some definite blessings you have received and "name them one by one." You cannot hope to name them all, but do name some. This leads to positive and constructive thinking. It tends to diminish our bitterness, disappointment, and defeatist attitudes. "Hallowed be Thy name."

(3) Naturally, the next step is consecration—"Thy kingdom come, thy will be done." As we think of the benefits we have received from God, we want Him more and more in our lives and in our world. We realize that it is better for us to have God, and we increasingly want Him to have full possession of us. Possessing us, we want to help Him possess the world about us.

So we pray that God will use us in His work. We begin to see things we might do to help, and we gladly commit ourself to those opportunities. Anything that we can do to bring His kingdom in we eagerly become willing to do.

(4) As you realize the greatness of God, you understand that all we have comes from His hand. That if God stopped giving for even one minute, every bit of life on earth would cease. We think of our complete dependence on Him. So we pray, "Give us this day our daily bread."

Back of the loaf is the snowy flour, and back of the flour
is the mill;
And back of the mill is the sheaf, and the shower and
the sun, and the Father's will.

(5) Then, when we realize that wrong within our own lives blocks out our ability to serve, and also feeling our utter dependence on God, confession comes next. "Forgive us our sins" is the fifth step.

Here we need to be specific. In dealing with many people, I have come to see that it is usually some definite wrong that needs to be settled. When we become willing to turn loose "that one thing," we usually have little difficulty in settling all the other things that are wrong.

(6) As we seek forgiveness of our own sins we are simultaneously seeking the forgiveness of every other person. Because as God comes into our own hearts there also comes in a deep and abiding love for Him and for all other people.

Here we feel the "expulsive power of a new affection." Prejudice, jealousy, hate, grudges, and indifference cannot live in a heart into which God has come. Thus it is easy and natural to pray, "As we forgive others."

(7) Finally comes the most important step of all. It is "Amen." That is a big and strong word. Literally, it means, "So let it be." It is a resolve of honesty. Obviously it would be dishonest and unfair to ask God to do for us what we are unwilling to do for ourselves. That word "Amen" is a promise that you will do all within your own power to answer your prayer.

Also, "Amen" means what Jesus meant when He said, "Into thy hands I commend my spirit." That is, I have done my best and now I am willing to leave the results to God. It is a pledge of faith and confidence. Thus, when one has prayed, his mind can be at rest in the assurance that God has heard and will answer.

Those seven simple steps are the "how of prayer and, when honestly taken, they become the pathway to power—power that gives light and understanding, a clean heart, and harmony within the soul.

16. Learn To Believe

ONE OF MY favorite stories is found in the ninth chapter of Mark. A father had brought his sick son to the disciples of Jesus to be healed but they had failed to heal him. The father had about lost hope.

Then Jesus came up and said, "If thou canst believe, all things are possible to him that believeth." The father replied, "Lord, I believe."

And to those of us who are defeated, worried, anxious, and afraid, Jesus is saying it is possible for us to succeed if we will only learn how to believe.

This principle has been proved time and again. Take football for example. The greatest football coach of all time was Knute Rockne. One of his first rules for the selection of players on his Notre Dame teams was this: "I will not have a boy with an inferiority complex. He must believe he can accomplish things."

William James, the famous psychologist, said the same thing. He said, "Our belief at the beginning of a doubtful undertaking is the one thing that assures the successful outcome of any venture." Notice he says, "the one thing."

If any person expects to succeed, he must first learn to believe. I say learn to believe because it must be learned. We had to learn how to walk. Before we learned, we probably fell many times, but we can walk now because we kept on trying after each fall.

Now, there are some simple steps that can lead one to the tremendous power of belief. It is not easy to learn, but as we learn we will see the magic of belief working marvelous transformations in our lives.

Notice that Jesus says, "All things are possible." That is the first step. Eliminate the word "impossible" from your vocabulary.

I have hanging on the wall of my study a large card with these words: "CERTAINLY IT CAN BE DONE." I see it every day and I know what it can do for a person. I wish I could put that card where every person could see it every day.

Someone has suggested a simple technique that I have tried and know will work. Start Monday morning and keep a careful record of the times you say or think that anything is impossible. Just before you go to bed write the number down.

On Tuesday concentrate on reducing the number of times you say or think something cannot be done. Write that number down Tuesday night. Keep that up every day, and by the end of the week you will have made marvelous progress toward completely eliminating negative thoughts from your mind.

In the church of which I am pastor, we often sing a little chorus that has become a great help to a lot of us. I find myself singing it to myself as I go about my daily work. It goes like this: "Only believe, only believe all things are possible; only believe."

Second, when you get those old negative impossibles

out of your mind you will slowly and hesitantly begin saying and thinking, "Lord, I believe." It won't be easy, because your mind will slyly say to you. "Don't bother with such silly ideas. It might help some people but it won't work for you."

But no matter what your doubtful mind says, just keep saying firmly and persistently, "Lord, I believe," and gradually the very pattern of your thoughts will become patterns of faith.

However, many fail because they miss the most important part. This man did not say to Jesus, "I believe." He said, "Lord, I believe." There is a tremendous difference here.

Here is the place psychology or psychiatry alone falls down. You cannot do it by yourself. The Christian faith uses all the principles and techniques of psychology and psychiatry, but it has so much more.

At the very center of the Christian faith is an eternal, all-powerful God. When one starts with God, putting his belief first in Him, it makes the major difference. You cannot do it by yourself, but with His help you can eventually really know what St. Paul meant when he said, "I can do all things through Christ which strengtheneth me (Philippians 4:13).

There are a lot of people who are defeated in some way. They are harassed by a feeling of futility and helplessness. But as the sun breaks through the clouds, bringing light and warmth to the earth, so this simple faith will drive the clouds out of your life and make you happy and victorious.

"All things are possible to him that believeth—Lord, I believe" (Mark 9:23, 24).

17. Believe In Something Big

I TALK TO people every week whose lives are tangled, and for whom living is a hard experience. Not in every case but certainly in a lot of cases the trouble is that they do not believe in anything. As the result of talking with so many people, Mark 9:23, "All things are possible to him that believeth," has become my favorite text.

Strong beliefs are to a life what roots are to a mighty oak tree. Fierce winds may blow, but the oak stands because it has roots to hold it firm and secure. The person who does not have strong beliefs cannot expect to cope with the adversities of life. So I spend a lot of time trying to fix belief in the mind of people who come to see me as minister and counselor.

There are many things on which I have opinions and notions, but the seven listed below are the convictions of my heart. They are my own beliefs:

(1) I believe in THE BIBLE. I list that first because it is the most thorough and reliable source of our knowledge of God. I know that the Bible is a progressive revelation of God and that it must be interpreted in the light of the day in which it was written.

There are some regulations and customs in the Bible that do not apply to us today. For example, Abraham had authority to take the life of his son Isaac. But the Bible sets forth the eternal principles of life, and they are as new today as they were thousands of years ago.

(2) I believe in GOD. He is the all-powerful creator and controller of this universe. There is nothing weak or flabby about Him. He is holy, perfectly good, and so He abhors evil. There is no instance in which He can compromise between right and wrong; neither can He permit me to do it.

He is a personal Father and I am His child. He knows my name, the thoughts of my mind, and the desires of my heart. He will help me in every way that I will let Him. The Psalmist said, "He healeth the broken in heart. . . . He telleth the number of the stars" (Psalm 147:3, 4). That is, the God who created this universe is a power available to me personally.

(3) I believe in JESUS CHRIST. He once lived on this earth. He lived a perfect life, and He so thoroughly understood the spiritual laws of the universe that He could work miracles. "Even the winds and the sea obey him" (Matthew 8:27). He could heal the sick and even raise the dead.

He was more than a man. He was the divine Son and the Saviour of the world. His death on the Cross is the only doorway for my soul into salvation. He rose again from the dead.

(4) I believe in PERSONAL SALVATION. It may come in a moment's flash, as it came to St. Paul. Or it may come as a steady growth, as it came to Timothy. Or it may come in a quiet decision, as it came to Zacchæus. But there is such a thing as a person being "saved."

I have a free will and I can accept and reject it, but I do know salvation is offered to me and to every person, no matter who he is or what he has done.

(5) I believe in the KINGDOM OF GOD ON EARTH. This is a belief that God is stronger than Satan, that love is stronger than hate, that goodness is stronger than evil. I have no sympathy with the doctrine that the world is get-

ting worse. I am convinced that when I line up on God's side I am on the winning side. The tide of His kingdom is on the way in.

(6) I believe in the CHURCH. It is not just another organization started and controlled by men. The Church was born in the heart of God, and today it is sustained by His mighty power. Beyond any lodge or club, the Church must have my first allegiance, and I do not begrudge one ounce of my strength, one moment of my time, or one cent of my money that I give to God's Church.

I believe in the Church prophetic, the church that has a message of authority and that bows to no state or ruler; in the Church of worship, that instills the spirit of reverence in the hearts of men; in the Church of service; and in the Church that is to be, that will one day lift men above all divisions into one great fellowship of love.

(7) I believe in ETERNAL LIFE, that the short span of years on this earth is merely a fleeting introduction to the next life God has prepared. Beyond this life there is a judgment, and some day I will have to face up to the way I have lived here.

There is a heaven and there is a hell. It is possible for me to live my life here and refuse to think of God and His claims on me. But every act of my life has an eternal significance. The sorrows, injustices, and hardships in this life will be compensated for in the next. The unforgiven sins in this life will be paid for in the next. I believe I will never die.

These are the convictions of my own life. What do *you* believe?

18. Guides For Right And Wrong

"WHAT IS RIGHT and what is wrong?" That is a question over which all of us have struggled and on which hardly any two of us would completely agree.

A great preacher declared many years ago: "Behind a great deal of our modern immoralism is not so much downright badness as a sincere confusion as to what is right and what is wrong."

There are those who say, "Let your conscience be your guide." It is good to listen to your conscience, yet a cannibal can kill and eat you with a perfectly clear conscience. A conscience must be trained.

Some people assert that a thing is right or wrong according to the way we think about it. But the Scripture points out that "the way of a fool is right in his own eyes" (Proverbs 12:15).

When I was a student at Young Harris College I enjoyed climbing Ball Mountain. Late one afternoon a friend and I were hurrying to get down the mountain before dark. We had taken a shorter but unfamiliar path, and after some distance we came to a place where the path forked. We decided that the way to the left was the correct one. However, after going down that way about two miles, we discovered we were mistaken. So we had to trudge wearily back and take the other path. We thought we were right, but we had to pay the price for being wrong. If there had been just one little guide post at the fork of the path it would have saved us so much.

Along the pathway of life we come to those places where we are sincerely confused. And we may suffer the remainder of our days if we make a mistake.

So let me set up four simple guides that will help us decide when we are sincerely confused over what is right and what is wrong.

1. Would you need to keep it a secret? Things we need to hide are usually wrong. The great Phillips Brooks once said, "Keep clear of concealment, keep clear of the need of concealment. It is an awful hour when the first necessity of hiding anything comes. The whole life is different thenceforth. When there are questions to be feared and eyes to be avoided and subjects which must not be touched, then the bloom of life is gone."

2. Where will it lead me? Many seemingly harmless little things are wrong because they lead in the wrong direction.

One of the joys of my life is playing checkers. I have studied the "book moves" and have played with many experts. At the start of a game of checkers you are free to move in any direction, but once you have moved, you are free no more. Every move demands a certain other move.

Life is pretty much like that. One action calls for another action. A little lie calls for a bigger lie. We can start wrong in a little, harmless way, but gradually we get in deeper and deeper.

3. Which is your best self? No person is a single self.

There is our passionate self. We sometimes say and do things when we are angry, or afraid, or are under the power of lust.

Then there is our careless self. We just drift along, not taking the time or making the effort to really think.

And there is our greedy self, when we are thinking only of our own interest and disregarding the rights and interests of others.

One sometimes says, after having done something that later he regretted, "I was not myself." It is wise to be very careful when we are not "ourselves."

The Prodigal Son changed the entire direction of his life "when he came to himself" (Luke 15:17). That is, when he became his *best* self.

Within each of us there is a "best self," which is so much finer than the passionate or careless or greedy self.

Shakespeare rightly urges us, "To thine own self be true, and it must follow as the night the day, thou canst not then be false to any man."

4. What would the person that you most admire do if he were in your place? For a Christian this means, "What would Jesus do?"

It is not easy always to decide what is right and what is wrong. But if we sincerely want to do the right thing, these four simple guides will be a lot of help along the way.

And it is always better to do right.

19. Get God's Guidance

ONCE THERE WAS a mule standing exactly between two identical hay stacks. He was extremely hungry but the poor animal stood there and starved to death simply because it never could make up its mind from which stack to eat.

ROADS TO RADIANT LIVING

Often, we find ourselves pretty much in the position of that mule. There are two paths we might follow and we cannot decide which one to take.

Or, more confusing, there might be several paths. Or worse still, no path at all. Many times we dissipate our power or lose our opportunities merely because we are not sure what is the best thing to do.

Most of us sincerely want to follow God's will, but we are perplexed about what His will *is*. It would be very convenient if the Lord would write us a letter and tell us specifically what He wants us to do, but we receive no such letters.

The majority of the people I talk to as a minister are people who are confused about some decision they should make. So I want to point out two principles that will help:

First, let us do what lies clearly at hand today before we start worrying about things far ahead. No need to bother about next July until first we do what we know we should do today and this week.

I once went to a Negro high school to give a commencement address, but the best speech that night was made by the old Negro superintendent, a man who had lived long and learned much. He was urging the graduates to go on to college, yet he noted that not one of them could see his way financially. However, he insisted that they should start and he gave a simple illustration.

A very rough road ran from the school to the town. It was a dark night. But the superintendent explained that one does not need a great searchlight shining all the way in order to walk the road safely.

All one needs is a very small light shining one step ahead. When that step is taken the light moves up and reveals the next step.

So it is with God's will. Most of us know what our very

next step should be. Let us take that one, and then we will be delighted to see the Lord's light moving along with us.

I always feel sad when I read about the three women going to anoint the body of Jesus that first Easter morning. The Scripture says they came "at the rising of the sun," and there is no lovelier time of day. But they did not see the glorious sunrise, because they were worrying.

The wild flowers were blooming in profusion at that season, and that morning the flowers were shining their brightest because God had sprinkled them with sparkling dew. But these women did not see them or smell their fragrance.

They were worrying about who would roll the stone away from the Lord's tomb. When they got there, however, they found that the stone already had been rolled away.

So it will be with most of the things we are worrying about in the far future. To know God's will we must obediently take the steps He already has shown us.

Second, to know God's will we must live close to Him. When we grow indifferent, careless, and prayerless, we find we have become insensitive to the voice of God.

When I lived at Douglasville, twenty-five miles from Atlanta, I could hear clearly on my small set all the radio stations in Atlanta. But when I moved to Thomson, 130 miles from Atlanta, I found I could not hear many of those same stations. They were still broadcasting, and I had the same radio. The trouble was I had moved too far away.

Now that I have moved back to Atlanta, I can again get with ease on my little radio all the Atlanta stations.

The trouble with a lot of us who are confused about God's will, who are worried about the proper decisions to make, is that we have moved too far away from God. We cannot hear Him speak.

When we fail to read His book, attend His church, take

time to talk with Him and let Him talk to us, and when we let wrong come between us, sooner or later we become sheep without a shepherd.

Think of this marvelous promise: "The Lord shall guide thee continually, and satisfy thy soul in drough, and make fat thy bones: and thou shalt be like a watered garden, and like a spring of water, whose waters fail not" (Isaiah 58:11).

Just move in close enough to hear Him, and then follow Him a step at a time.

20. No Situation Is Hopeless

I HAVE BEFORE me as I write these words five letters that came on one mail, such letters as come every day. A wife writes that her husband is insanely jealous and is making life unbearable.

A school teachers says she has been teaching a number of years but has reached the point from where she can hardly go on. She is not well, and the thought of facing a room full of adolescents fills her with dread and fear every morning. But she must make a living and is untrained for any other type of work.

A wife writes about a drinking husband. He is a good man until he starts drinking, and she has about reached the end of her endurance. A mother tells me about her only daughter, who is about to make a most unfortunate marriage.

The last one is from a young girl, nineteen years old, whose marriage was unfortunate. Her husband has deserted and left her with a tiny baby. She has no one to turn to and does not know what to do.

Every day such letters come, and I try to answer them. There are several things that can be said of any seemingly hopeless situation.

First, no situation is hopeless. I understand that the Army Engineer Corps has a motto they keep before themselves: "The difficult we do immediately; the impossible takes a little longer." And that is a clear statement of the Christian faith. There is always a solution to every problem; there is always a way out.

On my desk before me is the most reliable book that has ever been written. Part of it was written forty centuries ago, but it has lasted and every year it is the best seller, because it is true. All through the Bible runs one great theme: There is always hope for a final victory.

Plant deeply and firmly in your mind such statements as these: "Commit thy way unto the Lord; trust also in him, and he shall bring it to pass" (Psalm 37:5). "The things which are impossible with men are possible with God" (Luke 18:37).

Think disaster and it will come. But when you read the Bible, you think victory and eventually that leads you to triumph over any situation. The Bible fills your mind with God, to whose power there is no limit, as you will see.

Second, be honest with yourself. It is so easy to slump down before a bad situation, throw up your hands and quit. But most of the time the trouble is not the situation you are facing, the trouble is in you. Maybe you are not entirely at fault, but if you will do whatever is necessary to correct your own faults, you will find yourself getting along a lot better.

Third, know that you are not alone. When one is sick

there is a tendency to become afraid, even panicky. But the doctor comes, and he is very quiet and calm.

Before you even have the prescription filled, you begin to feel better. In fact, the doctor often does more for you through his own personality than the medicine does for you. Your confidence and faith in your physician do wonders for you.

So, when you are afraid of some situation and let God in through faith and childlike prayer, you feel a calmness come over you. Then you think better and begin to discover resources and use them. You begin to do what you can in a calm, quiet spirit. And, more important, you begin to feel the "everlasting arm" about you, and you see the way out.

21. Help For The Aching Heart

IN THE WORLD about us there are many people with breaking hearts. People are called on to bear many kinds of sorrows and suffering. Because I am a minister, many people tell me about these hard experiences and I do my best to say something that will help.

One might say that suffering is caused by sin; therefore, one should repent of his sins. There are times when that is true and I have seen a genuine repentance ease a breaking heart. But more often that is not the answer.

At times a sorrow is an imagined hurt and exists only in one's mind. The cure is to fill the mind with constructive thoughts, but most of the time that is not the answer.

Or we might say that suffering is part of the business of

living. A little girl fell down on the sidewalk and skinned her knee. She said to her mother, "Wouldn't it be wonderful if all the world were cushioned!" But it is not cushioned and every one who lives must expect to suffer at times. But simply to tell you to expect sorrows and grit your teeth and bear them is not enough.

There is a primitive African tribe that believes that although God is good and wishes good for all of us, He has a half-witted brother who keeps getting in His way and mixes things up. We do not believe that, but we do believe in the devil. However, to lay all the blame on him does not heal the hurt.

Some claim that suffering is good for one, that it is essential to the development of one's character, that, in a "cushioned world" our souls would become flabby and weak. But neither is that a satisfactory answer.

I have told many people with heartaches to memorize and saturate their minds with these words: "The Lord is my strength and my shield; my heart trusted in him, and I am helped: therefore my heart greatly rejoiceth; and with my song will I praise him" (Psalm 28:7).

By "heart" the Psalmist means his complete self. And when he put his entire faith in God it set his breaking heart to singing again. Truly it is wonderful what God can do for a broken heart when one gives Him all the pieces.

I want to mention two ways in which faith helps. First, IT ENABLES ONE TO KEEP GOING. When you have a sorrow, the worst thing you can do is stop. To stop is to begin to brood, and brooding induces self-pity, and that always develops and enlarges the pain.

Four times recently I have flown over the Okefeenokee Swamp in South Georgia. Over much of the water I noticed an ugly green film. At one time the water in a swamp is sweet and pure. But it runs into a low place and stops and then stagnates and breeds all manner of unhealthy things.

So in a life. If you stop when you hit your low places, you begin to stagnate, too. But God is eternal power and as one fills his mind with God, that power actually flows into the person, giving him a strength to keep on keeping on.

Then faith in God does a second thing for a breaking heart, IT BRINGS IN LOVE, and love is the greatest medicine for the heart the world has ever discovered. Sorrows have a tendency to breed bitterness and resentment. When one is hurt it is a temptation to complain, fuss, and even get angry. It is a tragedy indeed when a broken heart turns sour.

But God is love, and when one puts his faith in God, love begins to flow into him. I do not know exactly how it works, because the human mind is far too complicated a mechanism for me to understand, but I do know that when love fills an aching heart, somehow, the pain goes away.

All of us are so familiar with the beautiful "love chapter," 1 Corinthians 13, in which St. Paul analyzes love and, among other things, tells how love "suffers long" and "beareth all things." But right up against that chapter I like to put Romans 5:1-5.

There St. Paul tells us that out of tribulation come patience and experience and hope, "because," he says, "the love of God is shed abroad in our hearts." Just as oil quiets the raging waters, so the benevolent blanket of love spread over a troubled life causes it to become quiet, to develop ease of mind, and to find peace.

22. See Your Opportunities In Troas

AN UNUSUALLY FINE young man came to see me recently with a problem that is almost universal. When he was a youth he dreamed of a certain career, but circumstances barred him from the career on which his heart had been set. Now he is disappointed and feels cheated.

There are a lot of people who have not been able to do the things their hearts were once set on doing. This particular young man wanted to be a physician, but he did not have the money necessary for his education, and had to quit school and go to war. Now his chance to be a physician is gone and he is filled with regret.

I read him a story in the 16th chapter of Acts. Paul had his heart set on going to Bithynia. That was the richest province of Asia, and there he saw his greatest opportunity. But instead of going to Bithynia, he landed in lowly Troas, a place to which he very much did *not* want to go. He was disappointed.

But Paul kept his head and his faith. He felt that God still had a purpose for his life, that even in Troas he could find something worth while.

And in Troas he saw the vision of the man from Macedonia saying, "Come over and help us." Paul obeyed that vision and in so doing was privileged to render the greatest service any minister has ever rendered since Christ.

Whenever I fly to Washington and pass over Mount

Vernon I always think of George Washington. There is the city below that he planned as our nation's capitol. Millions of people have seen the great Washington monument and given thanks for such a man.

But George Washington wanted to be a sailor in the King's navy; that was the dream and ambition of his early young manhood. Even his trunks were packed and his ticket bought to sail for England. However, at the last moment his plans were frustrated and he could not go. His disappointment was almost unbearable, but out of his disappointment came to him a far greater life.

When our government issued a commemorative stamp in honor of mothers the portrait of Whistler's mother was chosen. Whistler was the greatest portrait painter of his age, though, as a young man, he wanted to be a soldier. He went to West Point and flunked. Then he tried engineering and failed. As a last resort he took up painting and became famous.

Think of Sir Walter Scott, the "king of romantics," as Stevenson called him. His books are among our most cherished classics. But his fondest ambition was to be a poet. He tried poetry and he was a miserable failure. He was so ashamed of his first novels that he published them anonymously. He had his heart set on a Bithynia but in his Troas he found true greatness.

When you think of Jean François Millet you thank God that once a man lived who could paint such pictures as "The Angelus," "The Reapers," and "Man with the Hoe." The picture that gave Millet his chance was his "Oedipus Unbound." But the picture he worked hardest on was his "St. Jerome," and it was rejected.

Millet was so poor that he could not afford to buy more canvas for a new picture, and he was so disappointed that he felt like quitting. But he did not quit. Instead, he took his rejected canvas and over it he painted his first successful picture. His disappointment became the base for his success.

There was Joseph, the light of his father's life. Because of jealousy, his brothers put him in a well and later sold him into slavery. Surely Joseph must have felt many times that his chances were gone and that his life was ruined.

But to those same brothers, many years later, Joseph could say, "It was not you that sent me hither, but God" (Genesis 45:8). It made him very unhappy to be denied the privilege of his home and to become a slave, but he did finally realize that it was best.

One of the ambitions of my own life was to go to Yale after I finished Emory. But when the time came I did not have the money and, instead, I went as a preacher to a small country circuit. I do not know what my life would have been had I gone to Yale, but I thank God for the lessons I learned as a country preacher. I would not go back and change it now, even if I could.

But all of us have our disappointments, some more than others. Our hearts are set on certain goals and we find ourselves unable to carry out those fond dreams and ambitions. We wanted some Bithynia and have landed in some not-wanted Troas.

Instead of foolish regrets, Paul took advantage of the opportunities that come his way in Troas. Instead of whining and feeling sorry for himself, he looked for something to do. In the light of what he was able to accomplish, I know Paul was glad that things worked out as they did.

Finally, think of the Master. His Troas was an ugly, death-dealing cross. But He so clothed Calvary with the purpose of God that "all the light of sacred story gathers 'round its head sublime."

23. Count Your Dreams, Joe

"He failed to accomplish what he wanted most." That can be said of a lot of people but when I said it to a man in reference to Woodrow Wilson, he was shocked. President of a great university, governor of his state, president of the United States, one of the greatest statesmen of all time, brilliant scholar, well—one can hardly think of him as failing.

Yet the greatest ambition of Wilson's life was to make the League of Nations such a reality that never again would war be possible. He realized that he was unable to do it, and he died broken-hearted and disappointed.

Moses, the man who stood head and shoulders above all other men around him, also failed in that he never reached the Promised Land. He stood on a mountain and could see it not far away, but his own foot never made a print inside it. He worked forty years for that and he missed it. Moses accomplished great things but I am sure he died feeling that he had failed.

Franklin D. Roosevelt had almost the same experience. I firmly believe that as he looked toward the end of his second term every ambition of his life was satisfied, that he wanted nothing more than to go home and live a quiet life and write. Had that happened he would have come down to the end of the way contented and secure in a feeling of successful accomplishment.

But the war came and that changed everything. The biggest job of his life was still ahead and, whether we agree with his judgments, we all agree that he put all he had into it. And, like Woodrow Wilson, under whom he once worked, his one great mission in life was to see the war won and permanent peace established. However, his strength failed too soon. Even before he died, he undoubtedly knew he would not be able to see it through.

David, Israel's greatest king, had the same experience. The final ambition of his life was to build a magnificent temple. It was the one thing he wanted most, but this supreme dream was never realized and he went down to his grave feeling himself a failure.

This is a feeling that numbers and numbers of people have. We dream of grand and glorious things, we have high ambitions, our hearts are set on certain things we want to bring to pass, and so often we fail. Despite the fact that we have done many good things and have succeeded in most instances, still we are left with a sense of failure.

But it is both comforting and enlightening to read what God said to David: "Whereas it was in thine heart to build an house unto my name, thou didst well that it was in thine heart" (1 Kings 8:18). The Lord is saying that He doesn't keep books the same way we do. The world could not see the towering spire of the temple David wanted to build, but God could see it in David's heart and gave him credit for the accomplishment.

On a number of office walls I have seen this slogan: "57 Rules For Success. (1) Get Results. (2) It doesn't matter about the other 56." And we have come to measure life by that standard. Not so with God. He measures us not by our actual achievements but by our longings to achieve. Not by what we accomplish with our hands, but rather by what is in our hearts. By what we would do, if we could.

I think that when we get to heaven we will be surprised to see who God has put first. And many who received honor and applause on earth will go unacclaimed and unsung in the land where we are revealed exactly as we are. It is a very old truth but we often forget that, in God's sight, the person with one talent is in every sense equal to the one with five talents, provided that each does his best.

Once there was a little girl whose mother had been sick a long time. Mother's Day was near and she wanted to buy her mother something nice. But she had no money. All she had was a little china doll. Because she loved the doll so much she thought it was worth a fortune.

So she took the precious little doll and started down to the store to sell it, but in her hurried eagerness she slipped and fell and the little doll was broken to pieces. On Mother's Day, all she had were fragments of her little doll and the pain of her disappointment. But in the eyes of that understanding mother it was the finest gift of all.

A lot of people feel a very acute sense of failure, but when we remember that God measures by the "heart" test rather than by the "result" test life takes on new significance. It is far better to have a big heart and limited ability than to have unlimited ability and a little heart.

However, we prove the intentions of our heart by what we do with the abilities and opportunities we do have. Before John D. Rockefeller had millions to give, he gave a tithe of his first weekly salary—which was forty cents. Wilson, Moses, Roosevelt, and David proved the intentions of their hearts by going as far as they could go. When one has done that he need feel no sense of failure.

24. Things That Matter Most

MY MOTHER SAID something to me recently that I am sure a lot of other mothers have felt. She said that now all the children are grown and gone and she has a lot of time on her hands, she thinks about so many things she wishes she could have gotten for us when we were little.

My father was a preacher on country circuits and in small towns in Georgia. He never made a large salary and there were seven of us children. Suffice it to say, we did not live on the luxuries of life.

I always wanted a bicycle but never could quite get one. I remember how my brother John and I saved our money together to buy a bathing suit. We could get only one, so one of us would swim a while and then come out of the pool and let the other go in.

But I said, "Mama, I want to tell you about a man who had two mothers. His name was Moses." Both of his mothers were good and fine and did for him what they thought best and what they could. One of those mothers gave him a palace in which to live. She had an ivory bed made for him. She brought in the finest teachers of the land as his private tutors. She gave him wealth, position and prestige. His other mother was a slave. Her folks had been slaves for nine generations. She could give him none of the material things of life, but she gave him her time and her love and her prayers.

And when Moses became a man he had to choose between those two mothers. It was a hard choice for him, but the Scriptures say: "Moses, when he was come to years, refused to be called the son of Pharaoh's daughter; choosing rather"—his other mother (Hebrews 11:24).

Then I reminded my mother of what she did give us, how she read to us. I remember *The Youth's Companion*. It was a grand publication.

And she read us the classics: *Ivanhoe, The Old Curiosity Shop, David Copperfield, Tom Brown's School Days,* and so many more.

How excited we used to get over the *Adventures of Tom Sawyer* and *Huckleberry Finn!* We read all the "Miss Minerva" books. We must have read *Treasure Island* a dozen times.

Then we read Hurlbut's *Story of Bible*. There probably are better Bible story books for children, but I still like Hurlbut's best.

So I told my mother that if we had had all the material things that we wanted she would not have had a chance to do for us what she did do.

Suppose I had got a bicycle. I might have been killed on it. Anyway, it would be gone now. But so long as I live nobody can ever take away from me what my mother did give me.

Papa drove a Model T Ford and Mama would wear the same coat altogether too many winters. But, somehow, all seven of us finished college. They inspired us to go and, somehow, made it possible.

All this has caused me to realize that today in our eagerness to give our children all the things that money can buy we are failing to give them the things that money cannot buy.

This reminds me of a story that I heard some time ago. A mother was giving a party. She had a little girl six years old. When the women came to the party the mother put the little girl in a back room and told her to stay there.

The little girl stayed but she got so tired. After a long while she stuck her head out the door and said, "Mama, don't any of these women have a home?"

Somehow, I find myself thanking the good Lord that my mother was a woman who had a home. We didn't have much else, but, then, when you have a real home not much else is needed.

Finally, I read to my mother about the woman whose "price is far above rubies" whom Solomon tells about in the thirty-first chapter of Proverbs, beginning with the tenth verse.

Anyway, I think my mother feels better about it now.

25. Master Your Handicaps

NEARLY EVERY PERSON you meet has a handicap of some kind, but that is not so bad. It becomes bad when the handicap has the person.

For example, there is a story written by a physician about a woman who had a bent back. Her back had been bent for eighteen years and no doubt it had caused her physical pain, but, far worse, it had caused her mental pain.

This physician, wise student of human nature that he was, recognized that her problem was more mental than physical. In fact, in his report he wrote that she had a "spirit of infirmity." She had a bent back; the bent back also had her.

Reading between the lines of this doctor's report, one can see that she had let her handicap warp her spirit. She probably felt very self-conscious. When she was around other people she felt that they were thinking of her bent back. I am sure she developed a case of self-pity, even self-hatred. This terrible handicap robbed her of all the joy of living, and life for her was an altogether painful experience.

But the doctor goes on to tell about a strange experience that the woman had. She met Christ, who said to her, "Woman, thou art loosed from thine infirmity." That does not mean that Christ straightened her back. He might have. But it does mean that He freed her of the power that her handicap held over her. It means that He so changed her thinking that she could be happy regardless of her handicap.

The doctor's name who wrote that story was Luke, and you can read it in Luke 13:11-13. Luke concludes the story by saying the woman was made straight, and that, instead of being bitter and complaining, instead of cursing her fate, she became a person of praise who "glorified God." Through her experience with Christ, she gained such a spirit inside that the bent back outside became inconsequential.

Recently I have been talking with a number of physicians. There are no people that I admire more than medical doctors and nurses. One doctor said to me: "I have treated many patients with a broken leg when their main trouble was a broken heart." Another doctor told me that fully half of the people that crowd his office have nothing wrong with them physically. But, like the women in Dr. Luke's report, they are sick in their thinking—they have a "spirit of infirmity." And when one's spirit is sick, indeed they are sick all over.

And there are a number of physicians who are actually prescribing for a lot of their patients that they attend church regularly. Dr. Paul DuBois, one of the great psychotherapists of today, said, "Religious faith is the best preventive against the maladies of the soul, mind and body, and it is the most powerful medicine we have ever discovered for curing them."

I see a lot of people who have "bent backs" in one form or another. That is, they have some handicap that has depressed their spirits. And those people desperately need something that will lift and fortify them within. The thing that will mean most to them is to meet Christ.

It may be that when one puts his life in Christ's hands through faith He will remove the handicap. A woman came in to see me some time ago. She was very unhappy because of the place where she lived. She wanted a small apartment and could not afford the rent that was asked for the apartments she found. I suggested that we pray about it, and we did. The very next day this same woman phoned me. She said the strangest thing had happened that morning. She was walking down the street and saw a real estate office. She felt urged to go in and inquire about an apartment. They had exactly what she wanted at a price she could afford to pay. I know that God directed her.

But, on the other hand, He doesn't always work like that. In other cases God might have let the woman stay where she was. But He can give one such an inner power and strength that he can be happy, regardless of the circumstances. And this inner happiness will work to change the outward circumstances.

An old negro prayed, "Lord, help me to understand that you ain't gwine to let nothin' come my way that you and me can't handle together." St. Paul prayed that God would remove the thorn from his flesh. Something was hurting him that he wanted to be rid of. But God did not remove the thorn. Instead, He said, "My grace is sufficient for thee" (2 Corinthians 12:9).

Faith gives to one an inner strength that makes him sufficient to cope with any circumstance or handicap.

26. Handle Your Disappointments

DISAPPOINTMENTS COME TO all of us, and the more I see of life, the more convinced I am that one of the most important lessons any person can learn is how to handle a disappointment.

One of the bitterest disappointments I ever had was when I was in grammar school. We were having a Christmas tree and had drawn names, the idea being that each was to bring a present for the one whose name he had drawn. Each of us brought his present that day, and finally time came to give them out.

The teacher took the presents off the tree and called out the names. Each time I hoped that the next present would be mine, but finally she called the last present and never did call my name. I was the only one in the class who went home without a present. What happened was the one who drew my name was sick and could not come that day. But I learned early in life that a disappointment can be a hard experience.

We used to sing a popular song that went like this:

> I'm waiting for ships that never come in, watching and waiting in vain.

It seems that life's stormy sea holds nothing for me,
	but broken dreams and golden schemes.
With each day of sorrow I like to pretend, some glad
	tomorrow the waiting will end.
I'm waiting for ships that never come in, watching and
	waiting in vain.

A lot of people can sing that song. I know mothers and fathers who are disappointed in their children. Many are disappointed because of lack of opportunities. One of the loveliest young ladies I know came and told me about the boy she expected to marry writing her that he had decided to marry another girl. Disappointments have broken a lot of hearts.

I am even sympathetic with the little boy who slipped under the side of a big tent, thinking it was a circus. After he got in he discovered it was a revival meeting. I know how he felt.

A disappointment is a bad mental wound. It cuts deeply and hurts terribly. And, if one is not careful, the wound that disappointment makes can become infected. Bitterness can get started there. Anger, hatred, jealousy, worry and fear just thrive on disappointments.

Disappointment can give a good start in our thinking to such things as discouragement, hopelessness, and a "what's-the-use?" spirit.

But there is a prescription that I frequently tell people about. If faithfully taken, it is a sure cure. Here it is: "Delight thyself also in the Lord; and he shall give thee the desires of thine heart. Commit thy way unto the Lord; trust also in him; and he shall bring it to pass" (Psalm 37:4, 5).

Notice some of the elements in that prescription. "Commit thy way unto the Lord." There is glorious peace and power in doing the best that you can and then trusting in

God, believing that, somehow, things will work out for the best.

One of the finest things I have ever heard came from a man who said, "I have changed my disappointments to HIS appointments." Whatever happens, he believes that God knows about it, and he just takes it and goes on.

Who is wise enough to plot his own future? We cannot understand a lot of things right here in the present. Why do we assume the enormous assumption that we have the wisdom to plot our future?

It is sometimes hard to see God's hand in some things that happen; you may not understand today why it happened that way. It may take a year or maybe even twenty years, but, if you keep your faith, eventually you will see that things do happen for the best. God will "give thee the desires of thine heart."

"Delight thyself also in the Lord." Don't get sour and bitter. Keep a smile on your face, keep "singing in the rain," and, above all, keep going. Remember, "He shall bring it to pass."

I stood recently on a bridge over the great Mississippi river. I thought of William Alexander Percy's little book, *Lanterns On The Levy*, which tells about how the men would patrol the levies when the big river was at flood stage. The wives at night could look out and see the lanterns and feel safe, knowing they were being watched over.

Then I looked at that Mississippi delta land. And I thought of how time and again that land had been flooded and of how every flood was a disappointment to a lot of peoples. Houses were wrecked and crops were destroyed. But each flood left a deposit of soil, and today that land is one of the richest sections in all the world.

The flood of disappointment hurts, but it leaves life richer and better when it is rightly borne.

27. Wait For Your Easters

THE MOST VIVID portrayal of the trial, crucifixion, and resurrection of Christ that I have ever seen was on television one Sunday afternoon. Had I known what was coming, I think I would have turned to something else and not have let our two little children (aged four and six) see it, but after it started we decided to let them see it all the way through.

They see all the fighting, shooting, and killing in the wild West pictures, but that doesn't bother them; they know it isn't real. But this was Jesus! Since they were old enough to learn, they had been taught that Jesus was good and kind and that He loved everybody. They sing "Jesus loves me, this I know," and they have come to love Him.

They saw men whipping Him and it broke their hearts. When He was nailed to the cross, they cried. They had heard about the cross, but it had never been so real to them before. They could hardly bear it. Then He was buried, and I have never seen two more confused and unhappy children.

I told them to keep on watching and see what happened. Then Easter morning came. There were the women on the way to the tomb, feeling just as our own little children felt. But the resurrection came. He rose out of the grave and walked in the garden.

And what a marvelous relief and joy showed on the faces of those two little children. That little four-year-old girl gleefully said, "Jesus is all right. He has 'arised.'" The fact that everything came out so well in the end was all they needed to know.

Easter can be an ever-recurring experience. Many people go through severe trials. We are hurt very deeply. We feel the bitter injustice of many things that come our way. Many become confused and resentful. A lot of people give up and quit on some Calvary's hill in their own lives.

If only we would just be patient and keep on doing the best we can under the circumstances we would learn that Easter comes after Calvary. Read the story of the creation in the first chapter of Genesis. There we find it written: "And the evening and morning were the first day."

God's day ends with the morning. There comes into almost every life a dark night, and it is so easy to feel that is the end, that it will always be dark. But on Easter we know that Calvary is never the final word. And through faith we know that after the dark comes the sunrise.

One of the greatest thinkers England ever produced was William Cowper. Late in life he developed a brain disease and realized he was losing his mind. He could not bear the thought of it and decided to take his own life. He went down to the river to drown himself, but some people were there fishing and he returned home.

He went up to the attic and tied a rope around a rafter and the other around his neck to hang himself, but the rope broke when he put his weight on it. Then he went down to his study, took a sharp sword, stood it up and fell on the point, but the sword broke. Then he sat down and wrote these words:

> God moves in a mysterious way
> His wonders to perform;
> He plants His footsteps in the sea,
> And rides upon the storm.

Ye fearful saints, fresh courage take;
The clouds ye so much dread
Are big with mercy, and shall break
In blessings on your head.
Judge not the Lord by feeble sense,
But trust Him in His grace;
Behind a frowning providence
He hides a smiling face.

Maltie D. Babcock said it so well: "Some views of life are never understood except in review. Reserve your judgment. Time will vindicate God, and if it does not set you to singing, eternity will."

Disappointments, troubles, and heartaches come, but know that spring always follows winter, that morning always follows night, and that Easter always crowns Calvary! Such will be the experience of every one of us if only we will believe.

Dr. Lynn Harold Hough says that one day a man rushed into his study and told him that his only son had just been killed. He roughly took hold of Dr. Hough and shouted, "Where was God when my boy got killed?" Dr. Hough said the answer flashed into his mind, "Where was God when your boy got killed? The same place He was when His boy got killed?"

You can afford to trust God. He is well acquainted with the bitter experience of Calvary. But He also knows that Easter is not far behind.

28. Throw Away Your Walking Stick

"Found—a man's walking stick."

It was left hanging in the vestibule of the church and so far it has remained there, unclaimed. People leave a lot of things at church—umbrellas, handkerchiefs, scarfs, women's pocketbooks, men's hats, etc., but this is the first time I have known anyone to forget his walking stick.

It is a strong, heavy stick capable of holding up a big man. The rubber tip on the end is about worn off, indicating that the user kept a firm grip on it while in use.

But maybe it was not forgotten. It may have been discarded, the user deciding he would not be needing it any longer. The fact that it has been left hanging there would indicate as much.

It is possible that something happened to the owner while he was in church that night, similar to what happened to the man sitting at the pool of Bethesda that we read about in the fifth chapter of John.

There was a tradition that at certain seasons an angel would trouble the waters of Bethesda and that whoever jumped into the pool first would be cured of his ailments. For thirty-eight years this man had been waiting around there, but always somebody got in ahead of him.

He complained that it was not his fault that others had someone to help them and that he had none. Circumstances were just against him.

Jesus asked, "Wilt thou be made whole?" That is, do you really want to get well? When the man said he did, Jesus said, "Rise, take up thy bed, and walk." The Lord was saying, Stop waiting for circumstances to get right, stop looking for somebody else to help you, get up, throw away your bed, and get going.

And to his utter amazement, the man was well

In my mind, I can see the owner of that walking stick hobbling up to the church that night. Either he was ashamed of his stick, or else he did not want to be bothered with it during the service, so he left it in the vestibule. But without his stick walking probably was difficult, so he sat on a back seat near the door.

Maybe he looked around at the other nine hundred people there that night and observed that most of them were happy, well and strong. It is quite possible that the power of suggestion which came from seeing so many people who did not need sticks influenced him.

Being infirm, he probably got there early so as not to be pushed around in the crowd. He heard the soft organ music, and that may have had a calming, healing influence on him. I imagine that he was not the type to join in the singing much but, as the congregation sang the old songs he has loved all his life, he forgot himself and joined in a chorus or two.

I suspect that he was one of those fellows who has thought for years of his infirmities and, thinking of himself, naturally he has never given anything much. But maybe his heart had become so warmed by the service that when the collection plates were passed he made a contribution. We had a ten-dollar bill in the plate that night, and I dare hope that he was the one who put it in.

In the sermon, I talked about the power of God. I used as a text: "But they that wait upon the Lord shall renew their strength; they shall mount up with wings as eagles; they shall run, and not be weary, and they shall walk, and not faint."

It may be that the great truth took possession of him and he was lifted out of himself into the peace and power of God. I am hoping that, along with about six hundred others that night, he came forward to kneel and pray at the altar.

I do not know the facts of the case. But I do know that he brought the stick with him and I know that he left it there, and that he has not needed it enough to send for it.

When I was a student in the School of Theology at Emory, Dr. Harvey W. Cox, the president of the university, made a statement to us one day that had a profound influence on me. They had just received a large gift for the hospital.

He told us about the gift and then said, "If the young preachers of America would prepare themselves to do a spiritually constructive and intelligently respectable job, we would have only half as much need for our hospitals."

A prominent druggist said to me, "I firmly believe that only one-tenth of the people who buy medicine really need it. The other nine-tenths are wasting their money."

Instead of feeling sorry for ourselves, complaining of our misfortunes and hobbling around on a stick of one kind or another, many of us need to get acquainted with Him who will tell us to "straighten up, throw away your stick, and start walking."

We need to "wait on the Lord." That is, study and meditate on His word, practice the sense of His presence, develop a firm and reasonable faith, and let Him "renew our strength."

29. That Feeling Of Security

WHENEVER I READ the story about the farmer finding the buried treasure (Matthew 13:44) it always excites me a little and I think about how I would like to discover a buried treasure. It is true that money is not everything, but those of us who do not have much sometimes dream of having enough so that we could have the things we want as we go along and enough laid up to take care of us in our old age or if some emergency comes along.

The man Jesus told about was a tenant farmer. He worked hard but every year would barely be able to pay out. He had no chance to save anything, and at the end of the year the landlord might put him out of the house. I am sure his children were under-fed and poorly clothed. He could hardly provide the necessities of life and none of the luxuries.

But when he found the buried treasure he bought the farm. Now all of the crop each year would be his. There would be no landlord to take half of it. Nobody could ever tell him to move. When he got old, he could hire someone to work the land and he and his wife could live independently until they died. He had a new security that brought peace and happiness.

I talk with a lot of people who feel insecure, and it is a bad feeling. Those give-away programs on the radio are extremely popular because, if one should happen to be the lucky winner of the giant jack-pot, how wonderful it would be. The money would relieve financial strain and the winner would have a lot of things he had always wanted but never could afford.

Our American politicians have capitalized on this desire for security in a fearful way. One was going to make everybody a king. It seems that the candidate who promises the most is the one elected. But we are only chasing after the pot of gold at the end of the rainbow when we look for security in some buried treasure or expect the government to take care of all our needs.

But any one of us can have that wonderful feeling of security by simply doing two things. First, concentrate on your powers instead of your problems. I read the other day about a group of scientists who met to discuss the possibility of building a machine with the powers of a human brain. But they gave up the idea because it would be too great a task.

They said that the human brain has ten million nerve centers and for every one of those ten million centers there would have to be an electronic tube. You have a radio with five or ten tubes; think about one with ten million tubes.

It would take a building equal to a fifteen-hundred room hotel to house it. They said that a machine with the intelligence of an ordinary earthworm would require ten thousand tubes. Even if a brain could be built, it would cost millions and millions of dollars; but God made one and put it in your head. Yet we only use ten per cent of our brain power.

Then look at your hands. We possess many wonderful tools but nothing has ever been equal to the powers of a human hand. It is wonderful to think about what a hand can do. So, with a brain and two hands, all of us are pretty well equipped to meet whatever may come along. Instead

ROADS TO RADIANT LIVING

of wishing for a buried treasure in some form, we would do a lot better to start thinking how we can better use what we already have.

But, as powerful as a person is, there is a still greater power that we can also use. Whenever he became a little shaky, Martin Luther used to go out into his garden and sing: "A mighty fortress is our God, a bulwark never failing; Our helper He, amidst the flood or mortal ills prevailing." That always prepared him to face with confidence whatever might come. He knew that so long as there is a God, he could feel secure.

One morning I got out of bed, worried about the things I had to do. I had seven sermons to preach in three days and a lot of other things to do. I felt myself getting tired and it was the worst kind of tiredness. It doesn't hurt you to get tired as a result of something you have done. That is natural. But when you feel tired over something you are planning to do, that is bad.

But I left home that morning saying to myself: "The Lord is my shepherd; I shall not want—green pastures—still waters—I will fear no evil; for thou art with me; thy rod and thy staff—the house of the Lord forever." As I saturated my mind with the blessed Twenty-third Psalm, I felt a wonderful calmness and I thoroughly enjoyed those three days that I had worried about.

When we think of and use our own abilities with the assurance that God is also with us to supply whatever need we may lack, we do find that wonderful feeling of security.

30. Be Yourself

ONE OF THE most thrilling and glorious facts of life is that you existed in the mind of God before you were born. No person is here by accident and it ought to flatter you to realize that, as God thought of all the people He wanted on this earth, He decided that He wanted you. So He made you.

Everything God has made has its own personal identity. There are billions of leaves but no two have ever been alike. No two raindrops ever have been identical. And no other person has ever been made or ever will be made exactly like you. The print of your finger is different; you think differently, and you look different from any other person that ever lived.

One day a sixth-grade teacher asked her class, "What is here in the world today that was not here fifteen years ago?" She expected the class to tell her of some of the new inventions and discoveries. One little boy held up his hand. All right Johnny," she said, "what is here that was not here fifteen years ago?" He said, "Me,"

That was a wonderful answer. When that boy was born something brand new came into the world. It should lift any one of us to a new sense of importance to know that, among all the billions of people, there has been but one of me or of you. Each of us can do some things that no other person has ever been able to do. Each can make some special contribution to the life of the world.

Robert Louis Stevenson once said, "To be what we are, and to become what we are capable of becoming, is the only end of life." Jesus put it this way: "As my Father hath sent me, even so send I you" (John 20:21). That is, there is a purpose for your life. Each one has something special to live for.

Stamp that thought firmly in your mind and it will drive out all your jealousy. Jealousy is one of the most destructive of all emotions. It breeds hate, prejudice, greed, envy; it leads to gossip, pettiness, and littleness. Jealousy is probably the chief cause of an inferiority complex. It makes life miserable for you.

I see people every day who have abilities I do not have and who are doing things I cannot do. But when I realize that God made me as I am for a special purpose, then why should I resent the fact that He also made other people for different purposes?

The best thing for each of us to do is to get busy on ourselves. Somone asked Thomas A. Edison how he accounted for his amazing inventive genius. He replied, "It is because I think in pictures and never in words."

He pictured in his mind the objects he desired to invent. This picture literally took possession of him. Gradually it would sink into his subconscious mind, and, even while he was thinking of something else, his mind would be working on that picture. The subconscious mind has marvelous creative power, and day by day Edison got what he called "creative hunches," and marvelous results came forth.

Each of us should work toward forming in our minds a clear picture of the person God created him to be. God had that picture in His mind before we were born, and let us pray that "His mind will be in us." Ask yourself again and again, Why was I born? What can I best do and be? Get the picture focused sharply and fix it firmly.

Proverbs 23:7 tells us, "As a man thinketh in his heart, so is he." Ralph Waldo Emerson said, "A man is what he thinks about all day long." Gradually you become like your thoughts, and a happy, successful life is yours.

In the name of God who first pictured you in His mind, don't be ashamed or afraid to be yourself.

31. Getting Along With People

ANDREW CARNEGIE PAID Charles Schwab a salary of a million dollars a year. Why was he willing to pay a man more than three thousand dollars a working day? Was it because Mr. Schwab knew more about steel than any other man? No, under him were many men who knew more about steel and its production. He drew that salary because he knew one fundamental and most important thing—he knew how to get along with other people. If you know that one thing there is hardly any limit to the possibilities of your success in any area of life. Failing to learn that, your life will be crippled and warped, if not a total failure.

I have a friend who is a teacher but not a very successful one. In fact, he never seems to be able to hold a place longer than one year. He has a brilliant mind, he holds a Ph.D. degree and he has a genuine ambition to do a good job. He works hard. But he has never learned the important lesson of how to get along with other people. I know a minister who has now been pastor of one church nearly twenty years. His sermons are just ordinary. He is not an unusual executive, neither is he a very hard worker. There is nothing about him that indicates great ability, yet he is regarded as one of the outstanding ministers of the South. The secret is simply that he knows how to get along with others.

Knowing this principle, a lowly man can even control his own household, and that is no mean accomplishment itself. I read a book on this subject recently and I decided I would practice some of the suggestions. For nearly ten years I have been having a very hard time getting one of my boys to drink his milk. He likes to leave about half of it and now, with milk so expensive, I am determined he will drink it all, even if it chokes him. So many meals at our house have been marked by an argument and fuss over this one thing. That hasn't helped my digestion one bit.

But after reading this book, I decided to try a better way. At dinner one day I said, "Son, you are one of the strongest boys I ever saw. Why, your muscles just stick out." He was audibly pleased. "How did you get so strong?" I asked. "Oh," he grinned, "I guess I was just born strong." "I guess so," I said, "but I read recently that when a boy drinks milk it just naturally turns into muscle. So I guess the main reason you are so strong is that you drink so much milk." When he left the table the last drop of his milk was gone and we had peace—blessed peace.

Any person who wants to be happy and successful must learn how to get along with others. Here are five simple rules that work for all who try them. They are not original with me. I have read a lot along this line, have observed many successful people, and these seem to be the five fundamental rules.

(1) Get interested in other people. You can win more friends in a month by being interested in them than in ten years by trying to get them interested in you. Instead of boring people about the details of your operation or children, ask them to tell you the details of theirs. Instead of

talking about your vacation, find out what the other person did on his.

(2) Do not criticize anybody about anything. When you criticize a person he immediately sets up a defense mechanism against you. He will begin to pick out the things about you he does not like, and emphasize them, and end up by not liking you.

(3) Do your work and forget about who gets the credit. Longfellow once said, "The talent of success is nothing more than doing what you can well, and doing whatever you do without any thought of fame." People will appreciate your accomplishments, and thereby appreciate you, but only so long as you maintain a becoming modesty. Give the other fellow credit and he will love you with a passion.

(4) Meet criticism from others with a smile and good will. In the 15th Psalm, David asks this question, "Lord, who shall abide in thy tabernacle?" Among others, he says, "He that backbiteth not with his tongue." No person can continue to hold a grudge against you unless that grudge is at least partly returned.

(5) Learn to get along with yourself. More often than not, conflicts between ourselves and others spring from a conflict within ourselves. When you have an emotional conflict, then everybody you meet will probably be a bit upsetting to you. Settle your inner personal arguments and disturbances and get at peace with yourself, then peace with others becomes natural and easy.

The ability to get along with others is, to my mind, the most precious talent any person can possess. It will do more for you than anything I know. Furthermore, it is the supreme sign of your religion, for Christ said, "By this shall all men know that ye are my disciples, if you love one another." John said, "If any man say, I love God, and hateth his brother he is a liar."

32. The Life Inside

DRESSING UP THE Christmas tree every year is a great experience. When I was a boy we used long popcorn strings. That was not so fancy, but I thought at the time it made a mighty pretty tree.

To decorate our trees today we use all kinds of gay lights, tinsel, artificial snow and icicles, colored bulbs and an electric star in the top. It is a glowing thing.

But when God decorates a tree He does it differently. Take an apple tree, for example. He doesn't come down some night and tie a lot of leaves and blossoms on His tree. Instead, He sends the sunshine and rain and puts food in the good earth, and the tree develops a healthy and vigorous life *inside*. Then the leaves, blossoms, and apples just come naturally.

And it is a good time to think about the best way to dress up a life. You might call it the development of your personality.

The old Pharisees insisted on the Christmas tree method —a tacking on from the outside process. They kept adding all kinds of laws and regulations of things one must and must not do.

Today we have personality experts, charm schools, and "self-help" books. But they are neither new nor modern. They are simply a carry-over of that old Pharisaism.

The greatest student of human nature who ever lived

told these Pharisees they were going about it in the wrong way. He wanted people to live the good life, too. In fact, He came to fulfil the law. But you can't develop this good life by just adding more things to do and not to do.

"Whatsoever things are true . . . honest . . . just . . . pure . . . lovely . . . of good report . . . think on these things." Plant such things firmly and deep in your thinking. Let them drive the unlovely things out of your mind and you need not be concerned about developing a lovable and winsome personality. It will come naturally, the apple tree method.

One summer I was teaching a class in which there were a number of ministers. Several suggested that we might spend two or three periods discussing the art of public speaking.

But you don't learn public speaking that way. Develop some deep convictions. Feel strongly some things you want to express and you will say them, all right.

Two men once repeated the Twenty-third Psalm before a vast audience. One was a polished orator, trained in speech technique and drama. He repeated the psalm in a powerful way. When he finished, the audience cheered and asked for an encore that they might hear his wonderful voice again.

Then the other man, who was much older, repeated the same words—"The Lord is my shepherd; I shall not want. . . ." But when he finished no sound came from that vast audience. Instead, the people seemed to be in a spirit of prayer.

Then the polished orator stood and said, "Friends, I wish to make an explanation. You asked me to come back and repeat the psalm. But you remained reverently silent when my friend had finished. Here is the difference between us— I know the Psalm but he knows the Shepherd."

I have heard singers get up in church and try to impress people with their voice and technique. They leave me cold and disgusted. But when someone sings who really knows the Saviour, though the song be very simple and though he is not a great singer, my heart is warmed when I hear him.

One of the greatest spiritual geniuses of all time was Dr. Henry Drummond. In reference to this business of personality development, he said, "It is the most astounding thing what happened to a tax gatherer, a fisherman, a farmer and a small business man—the disciples—when they lived with Jesus. They were transformed as the marvelous alchemy of His spirit had its way with them."

More influential than any living person today is a little, sickly man named Paul who lived centuries ago. But the impact of his personality grows stronger every year.

His secret was the apple tree method. "I live," he says. But then he corrects himself—"Yet not I but Christ liveth in me." He got the life inside. He continues to live.

33. Have A Plan

BENJAMIN FRANKLIN, ONE of the wisest men America has produced, said that early in his life he decided that the reason so many people fail is because they have no plan. They muddle through life, hoping for the best and usually getting the worst.

My own personal observation certainly confirms that. The successful people have clearly established the goals they desired to reach and then have followed some intelligent plan toward the attainment of those goals. The first step toward success is clearly fixing in your mind a clear picture of exactly what you want.

Then, in Hebrews 12:1 you find a perfect plan that, if faithfully followed, will gradually but surely change your mental picture into a reality. It is: "Wherefore, seeing we are compassed about with so great a cloud of witnesses, let us lay aside every weight, and the sin which doth so easily beset us, and let us run with patience the race that is set before us. Looking unto Jesus the author and finisher of our faith."

Notice the four elements of that plan: (1) "Compassed about with witnesses." That is a very scientific statement. It is a tried and proven law. In simple language it means that what has been done can be done again.

The book of Hebrews was written to a group of people who were having a hard time. In the eleventh chapter the author calls the roll of a great number of people who succeeded under severe difficulties, and then he says, Wherefore we have these witnesses, take heart in your present circumstances. They did it and so can you.

If you feel defeated for any reason, just look around you. You will find many people who faced the same conditions you face, yet have come out all right. What has been done can be done again.

(2) "Lay aside every weight." That is, get rid of the things that stand in your way, such as an undisciplined temper, jealousy, ill will and hostility, uncontrolled desires, or whatever may weigh you down.

One of the most common weights people carry is the memory of past defeats and failures. We must learn that no matter what has happened in the past, we can start all over again and look to a brighter tomorrow.

Above all other stories, I love to read about the Prodigal

Son in the fifteenth chapter of St. Luke. That boy made mistakes. He thought he knew everything and that he was fully capable of running his life without anybody's help. But he lost out and went down. Sometimes God lets one get flat on his back so that he will look up. That boy thought of his father, came back home, and started again.

Remember, others have been burdened by the same things that are holding you back. They got rid of them and so can you.

(3) "Run with patience." I have talked to people who have been years getting into the shape they are in, and then they expect the minister to give them some little magic formula that will change everything in five minutes. It just isn't done that way. Don't get the idea you can sit down with a counselor, answer a few simple questions, and walk out with a new personality. He probably can help you see some of your mistakes and point out some pathways to follow, but you are going to have to work and work for weeks and months, maybe for years.

But patience does not mean that you are to sit down and fold your hands. Notice the words are: "*Run* with patience." Get started immediately and keep moving as fast as you can. Somebody has well said, "All things come to him who waits, but here's a rule that is slicker: the man who goes for what he wants, will get it all the quicker."

(4) "Looking to Jesus." The mistake a lot of people make is that they think about themselves too much. The most powerful and stimulating force any life can experience is to forget self completely and be caught up in some great enterprise. For example, I have seen people pick up heavy furniture in a house that was on fire and carry it out. Had it not been for the fire, they never would have dreamed they could do it.

Under the stimulus of a great enterprise to which you

have given yourself you discover strength and abilities you never knew before. And the most power-giving thoughts one can have are thoughts of God.

As we become acquainted with Christ, as we fill our minds with His goodness and His strength, concentrating on Him instead of filling our minds with our own fears and weaknesses, marvelous changes come about.

I said to a man recently, "Read the Gospel of Mark carefully and thoughtfully ten times and you will see a distinct change in your own life." He did it and it worked.

This is a great plan that will work for those who sincerely follow it.

34. Something Worth Fighting For

WE HEAR PEOPLE say, "I hate war," but the average person does not feel that way about it. War has its appeal. We thrill to the patriotic. One of our chief occupations is criticizing our government, but let some outsider say something uncomplimentary about our nation, and our blood boils. Somehow, as we see the Stars and Stripes floating in the breeze, the band playing, and our soldiers marching, our backbones tingle.

When it is two other countries fighting and killing each other, we do hate war; but when America is involved it is a different story. Then so many of us are swept off our feet by a false patriotism.

But war is wrong. The Second World War included all sins known to man—murder, lying, thievery, materialism, unbrotherliness, irreverence, wastefulness, and all the rest.

Any way we look at it, there is no justification for war. It is intellectually foolish. It settles no arguments but demonstrates only who is the strongest. Sherwood Eddy says, "The saddest thing is not that some ten million of our best men are dead, that the world is impoverished, victimized, embittered by hate, rent by division, suspicion and fear. It is that we have settled nothing, made nothing safe, achieved no lasting good, that could not have been better done without war." Men with reason do not fight. Neither do nations, when their people think.

There is even less moral justification for war. Recently, when I was standing in a Federal Reserve Bank, I could have convinced anyone that I needed some money. But no matter how badly I needed it, I had no right to organize a mob and take it. And when a nation takes possessions from a weaker power, however great the need for more land is, it has committed a sin. Our needs do not license us to steal.

Micah saw the coming of that day: "They shall beat their swords into plowshares." With him it wasn't merely a wish or what ought to come, but a day that is coming. Of this he was certain. And the ground for his certainty follows: "For all people will walk everyone in the name of his God." When people walk with God there is no doubt about what they will do about war. First, though, all the people must have the same God. In Micah's day Jehovah was the God of only a small group and one among many gods. But today Jehovah is recognized by about half the people of the world. We believe there is only one true God, and thus the justification and obligation for our missionary program. When I give to missions, I known I am fighting war in the most effective way. The day is coming when all men will believe in the same God.

But we must do more than believe. We must live in

harmony with His will. And that day is coming. God will one day capture the hearts of all men. And when men love God they love each other. "Who serves my Father as a son is surely kin to me." There are more yielding hearts to God today than there have ever been in the history of the world, and there will be more tomorrow.

But men have an innate tendency to fight. Fighting is an instinct, some say. God gave us that tendency and it will stay with us. Psychology says we cannot destroy it, but it can be sublimated or redirected. Normally it will go in one direction, but we can make it go in another. We can't forever stop the flow of a river, but we can and often do change its course.

Two great fighters were Napoleon and Pasteur. Both possessed an unusually strong fighting instinct. Napoleon's tendency went as it would normally go. He fought for possessions and power. Pasteur redirected his and fought just as hard and heroically against germs, disease, and suffering.

Peter had a double portion of this tendency. When the soldiers came to take Jesus on the night of the betrayal, Peter naturally drew his sword. But Jesus halted him. Jesus admired that tendency in Peter. That was probably why He chose Peter. God has no use for men who will not fight. But Jesus gave Peter something worth fighting for. And as the world gains a clearer vision of Jesus, people will continue to fight, but will become "soldiers of the Cross" rather than soldiers with guns.

35. A Little Honey

"Take a little honey." Those were the words of Jacob to his sons when they were going down into Egypt to buy food. They took many gifts—balm, spices, myrrh, nuts and money. But wise old Jacob added, "take a little honey" (Genesis 43:11).

Honey is sweet, gentle and kind, and without those qualities no person can really succeed in the business of living.

I know people who have taken with them on the journey of their lives ability, training, initiative, ambition, faith, and so many good things. Yet they failed because they forgot kindness. If they had just been a little sweeter in spirit what a difference it would have made.

I have talked to many couples whose homes have been wrecked, their own lives forever hurt, and their innocent children made to miss all the joys of a happy, normal childhood, simply because they forgot to "take a little honey" into their marriage.

All too often, even among very religious people a little honey is missing. A century and a half ago a very bitter pamphlet was printed, entitled, "An Old Fox Tarred and Feathered." Who was the old fox so described? It was John Wesley, the glory of his age.

Who was the man who wanted to tar and feather Wesley? It was Augustus Toplady, the man who wrote the stately hymn, "Rock of Ages." They merely differed about a point in theology.

One of the finest lessons people can learn in life is to be able to disagree without being disagreeable. Simple, warm kindness will work wonders.

There are some people who say that this is a hard, tough world and that if you ever expect to get anywhere, you have to be hardboiled. That kindness stuff, they say, might work at a Sunday school picnic but has no place in business. But kindness works everywhere.

Years ago in Philadelphia a man and his wife came into a hotel. There was a big convention in the city and not a vacant hotel room to be had. They asked the clerk for a room but he told them they were filled to the roof.

This young clerk was one who believed in kindness. So when he noticed how tired the couple were, he told them that he would be glad for them to use his own room that night. It was small and unpretentious, but if they would take it he would sleep in the lobby. He assured them that he was young and that one night in the lobby would not hurt him.

The next morning the man sought out the young clerk. He told him how much he appreciated his spirit and that he had what it took to go far. Then he said, "If you will allow me, I want to build for you the greatest hotel ever erected in America."

That man was Mr. Astor, and he built the old Waldorf Astoria Hotel. That clerk was George C. Boldt, who managed the Waldorf Astoria and became one of the greatest hotel men in America.

We might remind ourselves that He who said, "Suffer the little children to come unto me," and "Consider the lilies of the field," has lived a lot longer and built a far greater army than Cæsar or Napoleon or Hitler could ever build.

St. Paul was no sissy. He was a man among men, yet he did not forget to be kind. He wrote some words that all of us would do well to heed: "Let all bitterness, and wrath, and anger, and clamor, and evil speaking be put away from you, with all malice; and be ye kind one to another, tenderhearted, forgiving one another, even as God for Christ's sake hath forgiven you" (Ephesians 4:31, 32).

In a recent play one of the characters says, "I suppose that the most that can be said for me is that I've never deliberately done an unkind act."

At first that sounds good, but most people can say that. Few people have ever been deliberately unkind. The unkindnesses of which most of us are guilty is unintentional. We forget the things we should remember; we do not weigh our words before we speak them; we allow our moods to control our actions.

Kindness is a positive thing. It is something we must think about and cultivate. But I know of nothing that will open the doors of opportunity and win friends as quickly and as effectively as will kindness.

We need only to recall the old argument of the wind and the sun about which was the stronger. They decided to settle it by seeing which could make a traveler pull off his coat. The wind blew with all of its boasted power but succeeded only in making the man wrap his coat all the closer about him.

Then the sun quietly and gently sent its beams down and surrounded the traveler with its warm rays. Soon the coat was off.

On the journey of life don't forget to "take a little honey."

36. Paths To Prosperity

RECENTLY I READ a little book that set out to show that if people will learn the Ten Commandments and apply them to daily life they will be financially better off. That appeals to us, because most of us work hard for what money we have and we would like to have more. We usually think of the Ten Commandments as a set of laws prohibiting us from doing a lot of things we would like to do.

And when somebody comes along and tells us he can help us financially, we are ready to sit up and take notice. Of course, this is not a new thought.

The Psalmist said that same thing in the very first psalm. He says, "Whatsoever he doeth shall prosper." Who does he say will prosper? The one who delights in the law of the Lord and meditates on it. That is, if we saturate our minds with God's laws and take a joy in living as God said we should live, we will get along better, even financially.

There is no spiritual value in poverty. Some of the most radiantly spiritual people I know are people who have a goodly portion of material things. On the other hand, I know people who have been driven to bitterness and despair because of debt and privation.

A man came to see me who is almost desperate because he does not have the financial resources to meet the needs of his wife and little children. His wife is sick and she needs medicine that he cannot afford. His children do not have proper clothing.

I could have preached to him about laying up "treasures in heaven, where neither moth nor rust doth corrupt," but right now that man also needs a little treasure here on earth.

And the "Lord of the harvest," the God who made a world with all the physical resources that are here, surely wants His children to prosper. God made our bodies and He well understands that we have physical needs and desires.

One of the most appealing stories Christ ever told was the one about the poor tenant farmer (Matthew 13:44). The land was poor, taxes were high, and when he paid the landlord his part there was almost nothing left.

This tenant farmer had no security and almost no hope of ever getting ahead. But one day as he was plowing, he turned up some buried treasure. According to the law at that time, whatever he found belonged to him.

So he took the money and bought the field. Now he had a new security, a new horizon. He became a freer and a happier man. Indeed, anybody is happier when he has a little something. Christ realized that.

The point is well taken, that if we will put our faith in God and live according to His laws we will see that out of His great abundance God will meet all our needs.

God made the world. It is a good world and He wants us to have some of the worldly things. Of course, He doesn't want us to be greedy and try to get all the world, but He does want to help us have our rightful share.

But God cannot help us unless we are willing to cooperate. For example, here is a railroad track. The purpose of the track is to help the train get to its destination. But if the train decides it does not want to stay on the track, then the track cannot help.

God has said to us, "The track of life is my eternal laws.

If you will follow it you can go a long way and life will be a happy and thrilling journey. But if you jump off the track, then you are likely to become mired in despair and frustration."

Of course, we all know people who have become rich and yet seemingly have paid no attention to God's laws. But one can have money and yet not prosper, just as one can eat and yet not be able to digest his food.

To prosper means that you not only possess something, but also that what you possess is a means to a higher and happier life. In one year seventy-three millionaires in America committed suicide. They got rich, but they did not prosper.

The Psalmist said (37:25), "I have not seen the righteous forsaken, nor his seed begging bread." Come to think about it, I never have, either. Have you ever known of a person who lived sincerely as best he could according to the laws of God who ever had to beg?

You will find the Ten Commandments in the twentieth chapter of Exodus. Read and meditate on them. Seek to live by them. They are the real pathways to prosperity.

37. On Being Honest

I FEEL A bit sorry for the man who broke into my study one night. He went to considerable trouble to burst open a little safe I have, only to discover that I am disciple of Simon Peter, who said, "Silver and gold have I none."

It so happened that on top of the things in the safe

was a talk I had prepared to give on tithing. Across the top was written my subject, "Will A Man Rob God?" That was the first thing the man took out of the safe, and I am sure he must have seen that subject.

In the very act of burglarizing a church, it must have bothered him a little when he saw that searching question, "Will A Man Rob God?" It probably shamed him, because, from all indications, he left immediately and took nothing with him. He may even be worrying about it, but if there is any comfort in knowing that there are others worse than he, I would like to point out to that fellow that there are thousands of people who would never think of burglarizing a church and who would sentence him to a term in the penitentiary, yet who are far more guilty of robbing God than he is. At least, this man knows and admits he is a thief. But there are many self-righteous people who boast of their honesty but are much worse thieves.

Someone has pointed out that the difference between South America and North America was that "men went to South America in search of gold and to North America in search of God." As we study the history of our nation, we cannot but see that it was built by men who believed in God and that those sturdy pioneers took care to build a church wherever they went.

Above and beyond any other influence in America has been the church. We sing,

> Our Fathers' God, to Thee,
> Author of liberty,
> To Thee we sing; Long may our land be bright
> With freedom's holy light;
> Protect us by Thy might, Great God, our King.

That is the faith that gave us the greatest land on earth.

We have seen it happen in other lands. When the churches are closed, the land becomes an unfit and an unsafe place in which to live. It would be so in America. And when any person lives in this land of ours, enjoying all the benefits of our society, and makes no contribution in time, effort and money to the support of the church, the one institution dedicated to the principle of building a free and wholesome society for all men, that person is actually guilty of robbing God. Like the priest and the Levite in the story of the Good Samaritan, he does not actually steal anything, but he sees a need and an opportunity and "passes by on the other side." To fail to recognize our obligations to society is to be guilty of dishonesty.

Not only do such people fail to do their part, but the greater tragedy is that they cheat themselves out of so much. God has said, "Give me a tithe and prove me now herewith, if I will not open you the windows of heaven, and pour you out a blessing, that there shall not be room enough to receive it" (Malachi 3:10).

When I started out to make my own living, my first year's salary was $410. I gave a tenth of that to the Lord. I have done it every year since. I do not care to argue with anybody about it, I just want to testify that it pays. It pays in peace of mind and conscience, and it pays financially. I have never known a person to tithe who did not feel it was a great blessing to his own life.

The basis of the large majority of our personal problems is selfishness and self-centeredness. I have talked to numbers of people who were nervous, worried, and afraid. Not in every case, but certainly in the majority of cases, what these people need to do is lose themselves in something greater than themselves.

Many of the emotional wrecks today are people who have gone through life thinking and living selfishly. The wisest man this earth has ever known said, "He that loseth his life for my sake shall find it" (Matthew 10:39). For a proof of that just look around at the people you know.

Do you know a selfish person who is really happy? Have you ever known a person who consistently has given a tenth in the service of God and humanity who regretted it or felt that he had lost anything by it? The dividends that God pays on the investments we make in His kingdom are the highest dividends paid in America today.

The hand that is closed in self-centered selfishness is also incapable of receiving the blessings that God is anxious to pour out upon us.

"Will a man rob God?" Yes, but it is a mistake to do it. We thereby are robbing ourselves of far, far more.

38. It Is Better To Grow Old Than To Shrink Younger

SOME PEOPLE SEEM to resent the fact that they are growing old. They hide their age in every possible way. Yet it would be a lot worse if, instead of older, we were steadily getting younger.

Just suppose the process were reversed. You would start living at an old age and every day be a little younger. Now that would be terrible. Every day you would know a little less than you knew the day before. You would start off with your grandchildren but in a few years they would all be gone. Your family, instead of growing, would constantly be diminishing. You would eventually get to the age where you start to college. You would start off a senior and end up in the first grade. Now, little first graders are cute with their short pants or little pink dresses, but I would hate to think I would have to be one again.

Tottering old age has its drawbacks but being a tiny baby is a lot worse. If you were getting younger, you would have to look forward to losing everything and end up by being a helpless baby with a bottle. Finally, you would just fade away into nothing. Babies do not have a previous existence, so complete oblivion would be the end.

No, I had rather grow older, gain by my experiences, keep up with the progress of this world and look forward to a world where I will continue to live. The Lord knew what He was doing when He fixed things. He gave us the very best possible plan for life. Each day our life is richer. We know more, our experiences are wider, we have had chances to make more friends, we are more efficient and capable.

I started as a pastor eighteen years ago. People who don't think much of my ability now ought to have heard me when I first started. I can do a better job now than I could do when I started. And when I am fifty, I expect to be doing better than I am now. It occurs to me that I ought to have a lot more sense at seventy than I have now. I know I am not as good as I ought to be, but I also know I am a lot better than I used to be, and I expect to keep on growing in my faith. Certainly all of us have pretty much that same experience.

To get older means I am growing; thus we use the term "growing old." To get young would mean that I am shrinking up. One cannot grow younger, he would shrink younger. So it suits me just to keep on getting older, and the older I get, the better it will suit me. I will not be bitter about it.

39. Aid To Your Memory

To AID MY memory, I have developed the habit of writing notes to myself. On my desk I always keep a note pad on which I scribble notes, such as, visit So and So, write such and such a letter, attend that meeting, and so on. And long ago I found that I needed aids to prompt my memory about even the supreme things of life. On the walls of my study are pictures that remind me of Christ. In my home are pictures of Him. Where I live and work I want something that will not let me forget the biggest thing in my life —my relationship to God.

Then there are pictures in our hearts. A man was in his attic looking through some old keepsakes. He ran across a picture of a little boy of ten years—his own picture. As he looked into that boy's face he muttered, "I have not kept faith with that boy. I have not lived up to his ideals and dreams." Down in your heart is the picture of a lad. Have you made the man he expected you to make? It is enough to bring any one of us to our knees.

There is the church building. When people build a lovely building and dedicate it to God, there are always those with the blindness even of Judas, who said, "Why all this waste?" Yet merely the building standing prominently in a community serves to remind people of God, and, in so doing, is worth all that it costs and more. As we take part in the beautiful acts of the service of the church, share in its consecrated teaching and lofty worship services, we are called to remember.

Because life is so full these days, none of us can afford to go through the day without a definite time for the reading of God's word and a period of prayer. And in those high moments we see Him, and the vision of our Christ will cause us to lift up our hearts and set our lives on a higher plane.

I used to live at Tate, Georgia, and I recall a story that Mr. Sam Tate used to tell. Years before, there lived an old drunkard in the community. One morning he told Mr. Tate, "The boys rocked me last night." Mr. Tate replied, "Well, Jim, maybe they were trying to make a better man out of you." And what a truth this old drunkard uttered as he replied, "Sam, I never heard of Jesus throwing rocks at anybody to make them better."

Sometimes it jolts our memory as some Nathan points out the ugliness of our sins as he did to David. But more often we are lifted as we see, not our sin, but our wonderful Saviour. Every person needs every aid possible around him to keep him reminded of the presence of God, of the beauty of Jesus. As we keep Him in mind there is a pull on our souls upward. Often we hardly realize the pull is there, but it is.

What do you have in your life to aid your memory about the most important thing in your life? You need aids to your memory.

40. Get Acquainted With The Christian Faith

WHAT IS THE Christian faith? Thousands of sermons are preached every day explaining it, and many books have been written on what a Christian believes, but the best answer has been given in just twenty-five words:

"For God so loved the world, that he gave his only begotten Son, that whosoever believeth in him should not perish, but have everlasting life" (John 3:16).

Martin Luther called that verse "The Bible in miniature," because it so completely sums up the Christian Gospel.

(1) First, it gives us a definition of God. There have been many words used to define God. "Holy" is the word of the Old Testament. Rome chose the word "power." Greece took the word "wisdom." Paganism used the word "mystery." Modern science uses the word "energy."

We might name a hundred words, each of which would define some part of God. None would be entirely wrong but each word would be inadequate. But here Jesus gives us the word "love," which is the word that most completely describes God.

(2) Then, here is the definition of love—"God so loved . . . that he gave . . ." Here love is not sentiment but service, not emotion but action.

This is a revolutionary idea of God. Previously, religions had presented God as a receiving God. They built altars of sacrifice, on which they placed their finest lambs and first fruits. Religion became a burden.

To many people today religion is only a burden. We are expected to give much merely in return for a dim promise of some distant eternal reward.

But Christianity teaches that true religion is not bringing our gifts to God, but rather God coming out of His invisibility to pour His treasures at our feet.

(3) What did God give? It is so easy to think of God giving laws that bind and restrict us. Many think of Him as a giant Santa Claus giving material things.

Emerson wrote a wonderful essay on "Gifts" in which he said, "Rings and other jewels are not gifts. They are apologies for gifts. The only gift is a portion of thyself."

"He gave his only begotten son"—a portion of Himself.

Robert Browning has a poem entitled, "One Word More." It is the story of a man trying to express his love for a woman. He tried poetry, prose, paintings, sculpture, but always he fails and longs for one word more.

Down through the centuries God had sought to reveal Himself in history, literature, prophecy, poetry, and through the lives of men. Then, in the fulness of time, He gave Himself. The love of God was made flesh and then we beheld His glory.

(4) Here is a definition of faith: "that whosoever believeth in Him . . ." Faith here is a personal thing. It is not acceptance of some creed, it is belief in a person.

The Christian is not so much concerned about *what* he believes as he is about *whom* he believes. I often get mixed up thinking about what to believe, but I get straightened out again when I start thinking about Him.

(5) Finally, here is the definition of salvation: "whosoever believeth in him should not perish, but have everlasting life."

The word perish here is the same word as is used when the Prodigal Son said, "I perish with hunger." We understand what that means.

To believe in Christ and His way of life, to follow His example, to seek to know His will, is to enter into life. Salvation means to live, to live on this side of the grave as well as on the other side.

There are five key words: God—love—gave—Himself—life.

Once I heard a man speaking of his great love for his mother. He explained that when he was a very small child he tottered out in the street down which were running a team of run-away horses hitched to a heavy wagon.

His mother rushed to get him but the horses were too close. She had only time to lunge forward enough to push him out of the way, and in so doing she was crushed by the horses and wagon.

He said, "I dearly love her. She died that I might live." That is the Christian Gospel.

41. The Inspiration Of A Greater Person

OLIVER WENDELL HOLMES once said, "Many people die with their music still in them." Any person who is in contact with people certainly knows that is true, and one of the questions I have sought an answer for is, "Why do some people become magnificent, wonderful people while others never seem to develop at all?"

I haven't as much time now to read books as I would

ROADS TO RADIANT LIVING

like, but I have marvelous opportunities to read people. I make a lot of speeches over the country and I have studied the reactions of people in my audiences. I have spoken in many churches of all denominations, at civic clubs, banquets, and conventions. I get a lot of mail and talk to a lot of people privately. And from my own observations I know that Holmes was right. Many people never develop.

Sometime ago a man and his wife came to see me. He had done her a terrible wrong. The wife told me the story and asked what she should do. I said, "I think you ought to shoot him. Have you got a gun?" The husband turned a little pale and said, "She's got two guns."

But then I told her that anybody can return evil for evil, get mad, and fly off the handle. Anybody can feel hurt, pout, carry a grudge, and spoil his own life. But some people have what it takes to rise above some things and become magnificent people.

We talked for a while about the forgiveness of God and the forgiveness of each other. She felt that she could not forgive, but she promised to try. We had a prayer together and they left.

Later, when they came back, they did not need to tell me. I could see in their faces that something wonderful had happened. She said, "It is a miracle, but I have been able to forgive." I stood in the door and watched them leave, knowing that she had become a magnificent person. And he, too, because it takes about as much grace to receive forgiveness as it does to forgive.

Then my question came back to mind, Why are some people so fine and magnificent while others are so little and undeveloped?

Certainly one does not become magnificent by trying. The more you try to be impressive, the less impressive you are. Not long ago I needed to have my picture taken. That always bothers me because I feel so self-conscious before a camera. The photographer told me that the main secret in taking a good picture is getting people to relax and not pose.

We do that same thing in life. We are tempted to pose and we spend a lot of time and money trying to look impressive. A lot of people put undue emphasis on their clothes and house and car. Many people belong to clubs they cannot afford and do not enjoy. But when it comes to being a magnificent person those things do not matter.

We are all familiar with the work of Charlotte Brontë; her book *Jane Eyre* is one of the most remarkable of our classics. George Richmond painted a portrait of her that many consider his masterpiece. He tells a story that explains that portrait.

When Charlotte was sitting for him one day her face was lined with despair. She was so lifeless that Mr. Richmond was about to give up. Then he happened to mention that earlier in the morning he had been working on a portrait of the Duke of Wellington.

At the very mention of him a complete change came over Charlotte. She had worshiped the Duke of Wellington since early childhood, and she began to talk about him. A new light came into her face. Mr. Richmond described it as a "strange light." He caught that light on the canvas and that explains his masterpiece.

What happened? Charlotte Brontë was inspired and became magnificent through the inspiration of someone else. Any person is at his best when he comes under the influence of a greater person who can lift him out of himself.

One day the most magnificent personality who has ever walked on this earth said to a group of very simple and ordinary people, "Come ye after me and I will make you."

As He walked with them He exuded some kind of a strange influence over their lives.

Today our choirs sing the majestic *Te Deum* that tells about "the glorious company of the apostles." And who is that glorious company? Why it is wishy-washy Simon Peter, hot-headed John, doubting Thomas, calculating Matthew, fisherman James, and the others. But He "made them."

I know of no surer way of becoming a magnificent person than by getting intimately acquainted with Jesus Christ and letting His magic power work in you. I have said to many people, "Read carefully and thoughtfully the Gospel of Matthew ten times and it will change your life." I have never known it to fail with anyone who tried it.

42. Faith Is Catching

NEAR THE CLOSE of his career someone asked the great actor Hobart Bosworth this question: "What is the greatest thing a person can have?" He replied, "That is easy. It is not money, because you cannot always hold on to it. It is not fame, because they will cheer you one day and sneer at you the next. But if you can have peace in your heart, that is the thing that really matters when all else is gone."

A lot of people think that if they can just get a new car or a new house or a certain amount of money saved up, they would be happy. But, actually, what we really want is to be able to be happy no matter where we live, even though we are walking, and no matter how little we may have.

I was telling this to a man in my study and he said to

me, "Where can one get that faith and strength that I seem to lack?" I told him that the place to get it is from those who have it. If you wanted to borrow some money, you would go to someone who has some money. The same is true of faith.

As a little boy, I used to go with my father to his churches on his circuit. During his revival meetings he always had testimony meetings, which were about the most effective services he had. He would say, "Now let us tell what the Lord has done for us." And one by one the people would get up and tell their experiences.

These experience meetings generated faith in a marvelous manner. Alcoholics Anonymous uses pretty much that same method. A man tells in their meeting how he was in the grip of liquor but, by the help of God, he conquered it. Then another tells the same thing, and still another. The result is that some man sitting in the meeting begins to feel that if all those could conquer it, so can he, and that is the beginning of his faith. It works both ways. Many times I have sat in my study all day long and talked with people who were tense, nervous, and afraid. And at the end of such a day I find that I, too, have caught some of that feeling.

On the other hand, when you spend time with people who are strong in faith and calm of soul you catch that, too. God transmits His power through people. We gain strength from each other. And that is the very essence of Christianity. As one comes to know about Christ and gradually to actually know Christ, he gains tremendous strength.

The fact that Christ is not here in the flesh makes no difference. Nearly every week I am in West View Cemetery in Atlanta for a service. I always take a few minutes to go and stand at my father's grave there. I think of him and I feel close to him. I think of his almost childlike trust in God, and remember how he used to pray.

His prayers were never very formal. He simply talked to the Lord as though he were talking to an old friend which, as a matter of fact, he was doing. He never had material things, but he had so much inside that what he had outside really did not matter. And I find that I get just as much strength from him now as I got when he was here in the flesh.

So with Christ. As I read His words and think of His life I find myself catching some of His spirit. And the more time I spend thinking of Jesus, the stronger I feel. This is what Paul meant when he declared: "In him we live, and move, and have our being" (Acts 17:28). Again, Paul said, "I live, yet not I, but Christ liveth in me" (Galatians 2:20).

Paul developed such a close comradeship with Christ that eventually he came to the place where he could triumphantly declare: "I can do all things through Christ which strengtheneth me" (Philippians 4:13). And that gave him that "peace of heart" that no outward circumstances could destroy.

The great need of many people today is to find something that will give stability and personal power, which, in turn, bring imperturbability of mind. Christianity has one answer. It tells of One who has exactly what we all want.

Christianity tells us to get acquainted with Him through the Bible, through the lives of other people who know Him, and through our own personal experience.

That is the only sure way to peace in your heart that I know of. And, unless we know a better way, it seems reasonable that we should try that way. It has never failed with anyone who sincerely and persistently tried it.

43. Use Your Faith

ONE OF THE things we need most is faith. Some people feel that faith is silly and put it in the same category as fairies, something beautiful but unreal. Actually, faith is the most practical, down-to-earth thing we possess, and we all possess it. Without faith one could not live a day.

I got up this morning and pressed the light switch—I had faith that the electricity would come through. I turned on the faucet and took a drink of water—I had faith that the city authorities had made it fit for drinking, so I did not analyze it myself. My wife could have put poison in my breakfast (and I suspect sometimes she is tempted to do so), but I had faith in her, so I ate it without question. I stepped on the starter of my car because I had faith in the battery. When I stopped at the filling station to get ten gallons of gas I did not measure it myself, because I had faith in the attendant.

I deposit my money in the bank because I have faith. I buy a war bond that will not mature for ten years, but I do it because I have faith. I mailed my premium on an insurance policy. I do not know the officers of the company, have never seen them, but I send them my money because I have faith in them. In the very act of mailing a letter I am exercising faith in the many postal employes who will handle it. I get on an elevator and ride up several stories because I have faith that it will not fall.

I go to the doctor because I have faith in him. I know nothing about the medicine he gives me, but my faith causes me to take it. I walk down the street without fear because I have faith in the people I meet and do not believe they would shoot me in the back. I plant seed in the ground because of my faith that they will germinate and come up, and then I have faith that the sun will shine and the rain will fall in sufficient amounts to make the seed grow. I work for my employer because I have faith that I will be paid at the proper time. I trust part of my work to other people because of my faith that they will do the work conscientiously and well.

I undertake some job that I have never done before, but I have faith that it can be done. I could enumerate examples for several pages, because there is hardly an act of my life that does not exercise faith. We all use it.

But when it comes to the biggest and most important thing of my life, my relationship with God, it is so easy to say that faith is all bunk, to say, "I don't have anything to do with this religious business. I want something real and practical."

The author of Hebrews reminds us, "Without faith it is impossible to please God" (11:6), and we might add ourselves or anyone else. Without faith life is unlivable. If you would build a great character you must first build a great faith. And really it is a very easy thing to have faith. In fact, you cannot help but have faith. You could no more quit having faith than you could quit breathing.

The definition for faith that we find in Hebrews is as good as any, "Faith is . . . the evidence of things not seen" (11:1). Close your eyes for a moment. Now, with them closed, you can see this printed page. Look now and you can actually see the door to your church, the pulpit inside your church. Look again and you can see your schoolroom, the soda fountain in the drug store, the face of your best friend. In fact, by looking through your mind's eye, you can see a thousand times as much as you can see through your physical eyes. And that is faith.

This very moment you can actually see Jesus. Look at Him as He feeds the multitude, or as He talks to Zacchæus sitting in the tree, or as He calls the Rich Young Ruler. Right now you can see Him hanging on the cross. Suggest any scene of His life, and you can see it through your mind's eye. And that is faith.

Here is a boy struggling through school. The work is hard and he has to make some sacrifice to keep going. Why does he stick to it? Simply because he sees himself as a man taking his rightful place in the world because he is prepared. From that mental picture of himself several years in the future he gains inspiration and courage. And that is faith.

Jesus said, "I go to prepare a place for you." Immediately there flashes on the screen of your mind a picture of that place, and you see life after death. And that is faith.

With these same mental eyes we see God. He does not have to be here in the flesh. And the more you are in contact with Him through worship and study and meditation, the clearer your picture of Him becomes. Look right now. Do you not see God? And that is faith.

So we understand exactly what the author of Hebrews meant when he said of Moses, "He endured, as seeing him who is invisible" (11:27). Open your mind and heart and let your own mental sight (or faith) lead you to the highest things of life.

44. You Know Enough To Be Saved

MANY MINISTERS AND church-school teachers have had the experience of leading some child to a Christian decision, and then had the parents object to the child's joining the church on the ground that they do not know enough about it. That same objection also has kept many adults out of the church who otherwise would have joined. Thus I ask the question, "What must I know to be saved?"

One of the most genuine and challenging conversions on record is the case of the Philippian jailer. The validity of his experience can hardly be questioned, and yet he was no theologian. He was a heathen who knew next to nothing about Christ. It is possible that he never saw the Scriptures of his day. And if he had seen them, he probably could not have read them. Paul and Silas may have been the only Christians he ever talked to. It is almost certain that he was never inside a Christian church. And certainly he did not have the advantages of a church school, with all its wonderful teachings and inspiration. And, more important still, he had no Christian parents to live the good life before him from babyhood and to throw about him the influences of a Christian home. Nevertheless, he would be a fit candidate for membership in any church.

One does not have to wait until he knows and understands all about Christ to be saved. None of us really understands electricity. Lord Kelvin, the foremost physicist of his day, declared, "If I were asked what electricity is, actually is, I should have to confess I know nothing about it." But while I do not know all about electricity, I am not going to sit in the dark until I do. I know two things about it: I know I need light and that electricity supplies that need. That is enough to begin on. I do not know all about digestion, how food turns into blood and bone and tissue, but I'm not going to sit and starve until I do know. I know that food will satisfy my hunger and give me strength, and that is enough to begin on. I do not understand all about Christ. It is something of a mystery to me how Christ actually saves a soul and a life. I have never seen anyone who could fully explain it. Yet I do know that when I completely dedicate my life to Him, He meets my deepest need, and right then salvation is mine. That is enough to know to begin on. One man said, "I had a thousand questions to ask God until I met Him."

Horace Bushnell, while a law student at Yale, was an unbeliever. During a great revival that was sweeping the university his conscience began to bother him because he realized that many undergraduates refused to attend the meeting because of his influence. One day he faced the question, "If I do not believe in Christ, what do I believe in?" He finally decided that there was an absolute difference between right and wrong. Then his next question was, "Have I put myself on the side of right, to follow it regardless of consequences?" He answered, "I have not, but I will," and then and there he dedicated himself to the principle of right. The result was that after he had been a minister in Hartford, Connecticut, for forty-seven years, he said, "Better than I know any man in Hartford, I know Jesus Christ."

Dr. Charles F. Banning relates an experience of Dr. John B. Gough. While a guest in a home, he was asked by the mother to talk with her boy. Upstairs in his room the great reformer found a miserable, degraded piece of humanity. "Edward," said he, "do you not sometimes regret terribly the life you are leading?" "Indeed I do, Mr. Gough." "Then why do you not abandon it?" "I cannot," came the answer. "I am bound hand and foot, and I will have to go on this way until I die." "Edward, do you ever pray?" "No. I do not believe in God. I do not believe in anything." "Edward, do you believe in your mother?" "Yes, Mr. Gough, that is the only thing in the world that I do believe in." "Edward, do you think your mother loves you?" "Oh, I am sure of it." "Then you believe in love, don't you? You believe that there is at least one good thing in the world, and that is love, because your mother loves you." "Well, yes, I suppose I do believe in love." "Edward, when I have gone out," pleaded Mr. Gough, "will you promise me that you will kneel down and offer a prayer to love, and ask love to help you?" The boy hesitated, but promised. After Mr. Gough had gone, feeling, as he said afterward, like a fool, he prayed. "O Love," he said, and instantly came a voice to his soul, saying, "God is love." Then he cried, "O God." There came back to him a verse which his mother had taught him, "For God so loved the world, that he gave his only begotten Son." Then the boy shouted, "O Christ," and the heavens opened and into his life came a flood of forgiveness and joy, and he rushed down the stairs to his mother to tell her that he had found the Christ.

I was five years old when I went forward on the invitation to join the church. Some say that is too young. I can only answer it was not too young for me. Because I then wanted to live like Jesus as nearly as I could. According to some definitions of salvation, I was not saved, but if you consider one saved who is dedicated to the best he knows, then I was saved, and so is every other person who has made a like decision. I believe God holds one responsible only for the light he has. Thus I contend that you or your child can be saved without reading another book, hearing another sermon, or learning another truth in any way.

45. Let Christ Change You

AN ADVERTISEMENT I saw recently claimed that in five easy lessons, and at a cost of only fifteen dollars, you can get a personality that will make you "click." I read the advertisement through, and it seems that the things one must know in order to "click" are: facial make-up, how to sit, walk and stand, voice modulation and conversation techniques, dress and grooming.

Then I got to thinking about Simon Peter, Matthew, and the other disciples. They were very ordinary men. A tax gatherer, fishermen, farmers, and small business men. They had very little education, and they had just about all the faults and failings of humanity. They were jealous, wrongly ambitious, hard to get along with, and very weak.

Yet Jesus said to them, "Come ye after me, and I will make you to become fishers of men" (Mark 1:17). He is saying He will make them into men who can impress and lead other men. He will teach them "how to win friends and influence people."

And the fact that Christ did it is well attested by history. In fact, those men led a movement that has actually changed the course of history. Cæsar and Napoleon are long dead, but these simple men whom Jesus "made" are winning more friends and influencing more people today, after nearly two thousand years, than ever before.

It is utterly amazing what the alchemy of the spirit of Christ can do for any person when that person allows Christ to have His way with him.

A modern-day illustration is Dr. Robert G. Lee, who was elected president of the Southern Baptist Convention for a third term. The story of his life is simply amazing.

Twenty-two years ago he went to the Bellevue Baptist Church in Memphis as pastor. At that time it was a struggling, little noticed church with one thousand members and a budget of $15,000. Today, under Dr. Lee's ministry, it has more than eight thousand members, and last year their budget was $350,000. Today they are in the process of building a million-dollar auditorium to seat the large congregations that come to hear Dr. Lee.

No church, or any other organization, grows like that by accident. There is always a reason, and in this instance the reason is the powerful influence of Dr. Lee. I wanted to know him and learn his secret.

When I talked with him I learned a lot about him. I learned that he was a country boy. That greatly encouraged me, because I, too, am a country boy, and I am glad to know that that is not too big a handicap. Dr. Lee was nineteen years old the first time he ever went away from home, and his formal education consisted of only a few years in grade school.

I learned some of his methods and techniques, but you find nothing unusual in them. The methods he uses are well known to most preachers. I heard him preach, and though he preached a good sermon, it was no better than many others I have heard.

I do not believe he ever had a course in a personality school. I doubt that he has ever taken time to read any of those "self-improvement" books. Yet I am sure he possesses the most captivating personality to be found in a city of 600,000 people. What is the secret of it? It is not to be found in his personal appearance or in the power of his intellect.

But that night, at the close of his sermon, I did find the secret. He was giving an invitation to Christian discipleship. But, more than an invitation, he was really giving his own testimony. He said, "I want to ask you three questions. First, Is Christ NOTHING to you? Second, Is Christ SOMETHING to you?"

Then he paused. I was sitting on the front seat and I saw the expression on Dr. Lee's face change. As he started the third question there was a distinct difference in his voice.

"Third," he said, "Is Christ EVERYTHING to you?" There it was! One day back yonder this simple country lad heard the call, "Come ye after me, and I will make you." He responded completely, he held nothing back, he yielded his life completely to the will of God. And what a commanding personality was made!

The glorious thing is that Christ's invitation is open to every person. He is saying to YOU, "I will make you." I have seen it happen again and again. I can tell you of women who were coarse and very unattractive who have become gentle and winsome under the power of Christ's spirit. I know men who were shunned by other men and now have become magnetic and influential personalities because they bowed in humility before Christ.

The answer is really very simple. Jesus fills a heart with love. And when one is filled with love, the things that are so repulsive, such as hate, selfishness, jealousy, littleness, pride, etc., are expelled. A loving person is the natural result. And when one is loving, he is also lovable.

46. Meet The Master

HE WAS BORN in a village, of poor parents in an insignificant little country. When he was twelve years old he was conscious of the fact that God had placed him here for a specific purpose. At the age of thirty he made public his plans and purposes and began the three short years of his public ministry.

He loved people and enjoyed being with them. He went to their parties; he was a popular dinner guest; even the little children crowded around him. He invited twelve men to work with him, and later he commissioned them to carry on his work. He told a ruler about an experience called the "new birth."

He offered an outcast woman water that would quench the thirst of her very soul. He healed the sick, raised the dead, opened the eyes of the blind, loosed the tongues of the dumb, brought hearing to the deaf, and caused the lame to walk. He fed those who were hungry, and brought peace to troubled minds.

He taught the people that happiness comes from the inside, that the solution to hates and prejudices is not in laws but in love. He told of the amazing power of prayer, that the treasures one lays up in heaven are more important than the treasures one accumulates on earth, that a divided heart leads to destruction.

Faith in God was to him a matter of supreme importance. Because God so beautifully clothed the lilies of the field, and because God cared so tenderly for even the birds of the air, he concluded that humans who are to live eternally should not worry about the things of this life. Instead, one should seek God's kingdom first and the other things of life would be taken care of.

He warned against people judging each other. He warned that a life built on any other principles than the ones he taught would be like a house built on sand that would not stand in the face of a storm.

He said that his kingdom was like the growth of the tiny seed that eventually becomes a tree, or like the leaven that eventually leavens the entire loaf. And that possessing him was worth all else one had, just as the merchant sold all his possessions in order to own the one pearl of supreme worth.

When one of his disciples suggested, after a marvelous worship experience, that he just continue there, he refused. Every mountain-top experience of worship was translated by him into acts of service and of living. He said that the way to become great was to become a servant.

Firmly he taught that one is never justified in holding an unforgiving spirit. To a crowd which was preparing to stone a sinner to death he suggested that the one without sin cast the first stone. And to the sinner he said, "Neither do I condemn thee, go and sin no more." He loved sinners and freely forgave everyone who would accept forgiveness.

Simple stories from every day life illustrated the eternal principles he taught. The Samaritan who turned aside to help one in need, the foolish rich man who thought of his physical needs but forgot his soul, the shepherd who hunted until he found just one lost sheep, the father who welcomed his prodigal son home, are some of those stories.

He wept with friends who had lost a loved one by

death. He was disappointed when some people he had healed expressed no gratitude. He pointed out that God expects every person to do his part, even though he has only one talent.

He cursed a fig tree for not producing fruit. He drove people out of the church who were misusing it. He said that we have duties to our government and duties to God. He praised a widow who gave a small gift.

He did not want to die, but he chose death rather than lower his standards. But as he died he prayed for the forgiveness of those who were killing him, he gave comfort to a man dying with him, he thought of the care of his mother, and he expressed his faith in God.

Three days after he was buried, he came back to life. He spoke to a woman, he encouraged some disheartened people, he spoke peace to his disciples, and one morning he even cooked their breakfast. He told his few followers to carry on his work until it covers the world, and finally he ascended into heaven.

He is today the one hope of the world. He is Jesus Christ, the Son of God and the Saviour of man.

47. Kneel At The Cross

IN BUNYAN's *Pilgrim's Progress,* Pilgrim was making his way from the City of Destruction to the City Celestial, with a heavy burden on his back. Finally he came to a hill called Calvary. He climbed the hill and humbly knelt at the foot of the Cross. As he knelt, his burden rolled away and was buried in a sepulcher.

ROADS TO RADIANT LIVING

Millions of others can testify to that same experience. Many people really know the meaning of that little chorus:

At the cross, at the cross, where I first saw the light,
And the burden of my heart rolled away.
It was there by faith I received my sight,
And now I am happy all the day.

I want to say something about the Cross, yet words are so inadequate. I feel like a little boy trying to dip the ocean dry with his tiny bucket. The Cross means so much, it's meaning is so profound that, instead of trying to explain it, we just kneel before it with deepest reverence and humility.

First, the Cross is a revelation of God's love for all men. Dr. Maltby, in his book, *The Meaning of the Cross*, tells of a boy who did many mean and terrible things. His father finally said, "I washed my hands of him."

Whatever the complete opposite of "washing your hands" of another, God did it on the Cross. We may do cowardly and disappointing things and bring deep pain to the Father's heart, but in the Cross we see that He never gives us up.

Even when the love of Jesus was thrown in His face with spitting and mocking and cursing, it remained unbroken. He is pierced but goes on loving.

Someone tells of a dark night when he was on the deck of a ship. Suddenly he heard a roaring and then a volcano near by burst into flame. The whole country round about was lighted; then the flame died. For a short time, he said, was revealed the fire that is ever burning in the heart of the mountain.

As we see the Cross, we see the love that is forever in the heart of God for each of us.

But the Cross did more than reveal God's love. Something happened that day on Calvary that forever makes a difference in the relationship between man and God. Something once and for all was done that day.

As a boy of twelve, Jesus said, "Wist ye not that I must be about my Father's business?" (Luke 2:49). He came for a specific purpose and on the Cross He said, "It is finished." Every task was completed, God's will was accomplished, prophecy was fulfilled, man's redemption was secured.

As someone has said: "There was no other good enough to pay the price of sin; He only could unlock the gates of heaven and let us in." His death on the Cross was not just another martyr's death. It was different from anything that has ever happened in the history of the world. It was something done once and for all. It had never been done before and will never have to be done again.

About the year 1830, a man named George Wilson killed a government employee who caught him in the act of robbing the mails. He was tried and sentenced to be hanged. However, the President of the United States, Andrew Jackson, sent him a pardon. But Wilson did a strange thing. He refused to accept the pardon and no one seemed to know what to do. So the case was carried to the Supreme Court of the United States.

Chief Justice Marshall, perhaps the greatest chief justice we have ever had, wrote the opinion. In it he said, "A pardon is a slip of paper, the value of which is determined by the acceptance of the person to be pardoned. If it is refused, it is no pardon. George Wilson must be hanged." And he was.

The death of Christ on the Cross is the pardon God has sent. Before it becomes a pardon for me I must accept it in faith and obedience. It is through the Cross, and only that way, that one can be saved.

His was not the only cross on Calvary that day. Two other men died with Him. One sneered at Him. But the other said with humble faith, "Lord, remember me." He was a man who had done mean and shoddy things, but because of his faith Jesus said, "Today shalt thou be with me in paradise" (Luke 23:39-43).

Fanny Crosby, who wrote many wonderful songs, such as "Blessed Assurance," "Rescue the Perishing," "Face to Face," "Close to Thee," etc., was herself won to Christ through a hymn.

In church one day the people were singing: "Alas, and did my Saviour bleed? And did my Sov'reign die? Would He devote that sacred head for such a worm as I?" She records in her biography, "During the singing my very soul was flooded with celestial light."

No person can explain such an experience. It goes past human understanding, but many know that such experiences do come to those who believe.

48. His Seven Words On The Cross

IT IS A stimulating and helpful experience to put before oneself the seven sentences of Christ on the Cross. So I am listing them in the order it is generally believed they were spoken by our Lord.

(1) "Father forgive them, for they know not what they do" (Luke 23:34). Jesus had very real grievances—the rulers had opposed Him and plotted His death, His disciples had betrayed Him, the people had chosen sorry Barabbas over Him, His trial had been unjust, He had been mocked, cursed and spit upon, His friends had deserted Him. But

when He prays for the forgiveness of "them" He means all of them. There is no bitterness in His heart. In a beautiful act of charity, He even excuses them and seeks to remove their guilt by saying they do not know what they do. This is surely a time for each of us to throw the blanket of love and forgiveness over those who have done us wrong—to wipe the slate clean by extending our own forgiveness and seeking even for those who have wronged us the forgiveness of the Father.

(2) "Today shalt thou be with me in paradise" (Luke 23:43). It was the word of hope for a wasted and misspent life. It reveals the heart of the Eternal that is ever eager to reclaim and restore even the least and the last and the lost. It is His word that this life is not the end but rather the entrance into a larger one.

(3) "Woman, behold thy son. Son, behold thy mother" (John 19:26). Even as He is suffering the agony of death He has a word of compassion and concern for one whom He loves. In the midst of more pain than it seems anyone could bear He still is anxious about the needs and well-being of another. Here is a rebuke to selfishness, a shame for hardheartedness. It reveals that we ourselves are living at our very best when we can turn away from our own sorrows and disappointments and seek to meet a need in a weaker life.

(4) "My God, my God, why hast thou forsaken me?" (Mark 15:34). This is the only question He ever asked God, and I believe it to be a very real one. It is His human side that is so clearly revealed here in a momentary sense of forsakenness—an experience that we all have some time or another. Every person somewhere along the way of life feels that God has let him down. It is well to recall in such times that the resurrection followed the crucifixion. Victory is always the last word with God.

ROADS TO RADIANT LIVING

(5) "I thirst" (John 19:28). Here is represented the physical price that Christ paid—the cost of something grand and glorious. There are no short cuts to the things that really matter. And, also, it represents His very deep thirst for God just now. In the midst of suffering even He who was so close is drawn even closer to the Father. Not always is that so. A sorrow makes us either bitter or better. But for those who will see and feel, God is closer in times of deep sorrow than at any other time.

(6) "It is finished" (John 19:30). Better than any of us, I think, can the boys who were at the front when the armistice came understand all that is wrapped up in those words of our Lord. The blood of the battlefield, the agony of the strain of battle, the homesickness in a faraway land, and then—"It is finished"—the victory is won. That is what Christ felt, only on a much grander scale. His task was finished. His kingdom was planted, and the "gates of hell shall not prevail against it."

(7) "Father, into thy hands I commend my spirit" (Luke 23:46). It was a cry of faith. He had done His best. He had given His all. Now He was willing to leave the results to God. And we, too, when we have done our best, need not worry or fear. God always takes care of the results. This was also a cry of refuge—even as we sing, "Jesus, Lover of my soul, let me to Thy bosom fly. . . . Safe into the haven guide; O receive my soul at last."

What great words to have before us throughout life—the seven sentences of Christ on the Cross.

49. Know The Living Christ

THE GREAT CLIMAX of the life and work of Jesus is the Cross. There He made bare the heart of God. There He performed that mighty deed which forever makes a difference in man's relationship with God. But it is the Resurrection that interprets the Cross, that reveals its divine and eternal significance. The Resurrection is the heaven-sent searchlight showing to all men their Saviour. Here I would like to discuss three questions. What does the Resurrection mean to God? What did it mean to Jesus' disciples? What does it mean to you?

First, the supreme value of the Resurrection lies in the fact that it was a divine act, by which God testified to His perfect satisfaction with the life and work of Jesus Christ. It is well to remember that the main question is not whether you are satisfied, but whether God is.

God sent Jesus for a unique purpose. He was to redeem mankind. As a boy in the temple, He expressed a feeling that never left Him: "I must be about my Father's business." He was sent for a particular reason. His work was different from that of any prophet or preacher. He had a special task to perform. And on the Cross, talking to God, He said: "It is finished. . . . Father, into thy hands I commend my spirit." He was saying to God, "I've gone my limit; I've done the thing you sent me to do. Now you carry on from here."

The trial was over. All the argument was in. A life that

could utter, "Which of you convicteth me of sin?" was the defense of Jesus. The Cross was the answer of men. There was one great judge. His was the highest tribunal, and from His court there was no appeal. The case was in His hands. What would His verdict be? What would He do?

Jesus was buried, and the tomb was sealed. He was completely broken and powerless. Then things began to happen. There was an earthquake. Angels descended. Soldiers became as dead men. Inside that tomb new life came into that body—a life so great that death could never touch it again. And the Conqueror of death came striding down the garden at sunrise.

The Resurrection was God's final seal on the work of Jesus. When He came on earth God welcomed Him with the voice of prophecy, the shining star and the singing angels. Then, after man had rejected Him and death had overtaken Him, the Resurrection was God's welcome back. God here testified to His satisfaction with the life of the man Jesus, the perfect work of the Saviour Jesus, and the complete victory of the King Jesus. It is God's message to every age that He accepts once and for all the way of salvation provided by Jesus. If perchance you are trying some other way, then hear this declaration from God Himself: "The way of the Cross is the only way home."

Second, and there were the disciples, the bodily as well as the spiritual followers of Jesus. What did the Resurrection mean to them? To answer that, it is necessary to remember how little the earthly life of Christ accomplished for Peter and all the rest. They could not understand His credentials, purposes, or plans. Seemingly, He was being defeated, but so long as He was alive they were always hoping and expecting the tide to turn in His favor. Then at Calvary everything crashed. Every promise was shattered into a thousand pieces under the rude shock of the naked cross. They had left only the memory of a beautiful life—an adorable but impracticable dream. There was nothing to do but try to forget and pick up their lives where they had left off.

Then early Sunday morning those women came running to the disciples, out of breath but with radiance in their faces. They had a message equal to that of the angel announcing His birth as they proclaimed: "Unto you is risen this day a Saviour." But the disciples could not understand or believe. Peter even went inside the tomb. "They've stolen my Lord away," they said, and believed. Back to the upper room they went and locked the door. They were trembling with fear. Then Jesus stood in their midst and showed them His hands and His side, and breathed, "Peace be among you."

Now they saw and understood. The light shone backward as well as forward. The life of Jesus now has meaning. It becomes a living thing, a flaming gospel. They are remade. From that moment on they never knew the meaning of fear. They went out to conquer or die for a living Lord.

> Then into his hands went theirs,
>   And into their hearts came He;
>   And they walk in a light divine,
>   The path they had feared to see.

And, third, what does the Resurrection mean to you? When Jesus came to earth He took the form of a human being. He had all our desires, hopes, ambitions, and temptations. He lived in a world of sin. Had Jesus slipped for one moment there would never have been a Resurrection. And thus in Him we see complete victory over sin. Therefore the chief significance of the Resurrection to you is that it demonstrates that within each of you is a power stronger than a whole universe of sin. You know that by the help of God you can make your life what you will.

This is a glorious certainty. It gives us so much to live for. But it also makes us terribly responsible. Every sin and every blemish in your life are there because you put them there. Every unforgiven transgression will be judged against us. At the time of judgment we will have no excuses, and, save for Jesus Christ, not even a plea.

Whether you face it or not, please do not say the Resurrection doesn't matter. It matters supremely to you whether or not Jesus Christ rose from the dead. It gives you the greatest hope possible, but it also brings the greatest responsibility.

As we see His life we know that because the victory has been won it must be won.

The call of Christ is the clarion call to the high life. Man can go on living for this world, leaving God out of his life. But God has a way of looking at people until they turn and meet His gaze. And when they do look up, the Resurrection is God's answer. He expects the perfect life of you, too.

But God doesn't leave us there. As we face the swift current of life we know it is much easier to go down than up. And when the going is hard God is for us, as He was for Jesus, a power at our disposal.

David Livingstone, in a hard place, once said: "I felt the down-reach of the Divine." And when we sincerely try, we also feel that glorious new strength—"the down-reach of the Divine."

50. Get "On The Way"

ONE OF THE most helpful and encouraging definitions of the Christian life that we have are the words Christ spoke to Thomas, "I am the way" (John 14:6). I think one does no violence to translate it to read, "I am the highway," which gives me a picture that greatly clarifies in my thinking exactly what being a Christian really is.

My study opens out on Ponce de Leon Avenue in Atlanta. It is a highway over which one can travel, for example, to Gainesville. I can get on that highway and start traveling north and I can honestly say I am on the way to Gainesville. That does not mean I have arrived at my destination. And there may be many who are far ahead of me on the highway, but, though I am far behind, I can still say I am on the way.

I might stumble in a ditch but if I will get up and start again, I can still lay claim to being on the way. However, should I stay in the ditch, or should I turn around and start in the other direction, then I could not honestly claim to being on the way. But so long as I am moving in the right direction I insist that I am on the way.

Now, a Christian is not a person who has arrived at a state of perfection. There has been only one perfect life and no other can claim that. A Christian, however, is one who has determined that the direction of his life shall be toward the Christ-like life. Then he is on the way.

In the first place, the Christian life is not free from temptation. Some claim they are not tempted, but they are mistaken. In *Pilgrim's Progress,* John Bunyan points out that even at the very gate of heaven there is a pathway leading to Hell. He means that one never reaches the point where he cannot turn into some wrong way and be lost.

But temptations are not sin. Every Christian at some time or another feels temptation. Temptations become sin when we yield to them. Resisting and overcoming temptations is a means to greater spiritual strength.

Second, the Christian life is not free from mistakes. The dearest saints have made mistakes. Our acts are the results of both our intentions and our intelligence and though our intentions may be the best, we will make mistakes, since even the wisest among us has limited intelligence. God does not condemn one for doing the best he knows, even though it may be wrong.

Third, the Christian life is not necessarily free of sin. I know some will argue that point, but where is there one who is without sin? E. Stanley Jones quotes a man as saying that Christianity to him means three things, "victory, victory, victory." But that is not true for the most of us. To many it means, "victory, defeat, victory," or "defeat, victory, defeat."

George Washington fought nine battles and lost six. But he won the war because he got up and kept fighting after each defeat. One difference between a sheep and a swine is this: When the sheep falls in a mudhole it bleats to get out. When a swine falls in he just lies there and wallows in it.

I spend a lot of my time saying to Christians, "Though you have fallen, still you can get up and start again."

Becoming a Christian is a birth: "Ye must born again" (John 3:7), and that birth is the beginning of a growth that must continue as long as life on this earth lasts, and maybe even in the next life. Thus Christians are at various points along the highway.

A Christian is one who has determined that the way of Christ is the best way and who has fully committed himself to that way. Some years ago I read a book on the life of Richard Croker, the one-time political boss of New York City. In that book it is pointed out that Richard Croker came to know Tweed, the then political boss. He studied him and in every way sought to live like Tweed.

And being a Christian means that one accepts Christ as his Saviour and in every way seeks to live like Him. If you would catch the thrill of the Christian life study Christ. Saturate your mind with the four Gospels: Matthew, Mark, Luke, and John. And as you see Him, seek with all your heart to make His way your way.

I now preach more times than there are days. Yet every time that I get up to preach, I feel like apologizing for my own life. And I do apologize. The world has pointed its finger and said there are hypocrites in the church. We have had to bow our heads and say it is so and I apologize for the hypocrites in the church.

But could I preach a million times, I would never have to apologize for my Lord. He stands before the world perfect, without a flaw or a blemish. And it is His way we are to follow.

51. Roads Make The Traveling Easier

HIGHWAYS ARE AMONG the most important assets of any nation. Find a nation without highways and you find a poor, backward, clannish people. Look at China, one of the oldest civilizations on earth, yet one of the most backward. One main reason for China's backwardness is that she built walls instead of roads.

Under David, Israel began her period of greatest glory and prosperity. David is known as the father of our highway system. He made treaties with the other nations around for the purpose of road building.

The saying, "All roads lead to Rome," explains in large part the fact that Rome was a world power for so long.

One of the main reasons America changed so quickly from a wild frontier land to the strongest nation the world has ever known is the fact that we built highways up and down and across the land.

The history of Egypt would have been very different had the Egyptians built roads instead of pyramids.

And as we think of the importance of roads it is very enlightening to hear Jesus Christ say, "I am the way" (John 14:6). To explain Himself and His mission, he used many expressions, such as, "I am the bread of life," "I am the light of the world," "I am the true vine," but none is more vivid than "I am the way—the road—the highway."

First, just as roads are necessary to the progress of a

ROADS TO RADIANT LIVING

people, so is religious faith necessary. I know of some communities which let their churches die, only to discover that the other worth-while things of the community also died.

Recently I heard a radio program which had been prepared by some of the leading scientists of our day. They traced the marvelous mechanical and scientific advancement of our generation and then concluded: "We have built a bright, shiny world OUTSIDE: but have failed to build ourselves INSIDE, and now our world is about to crush us to death."

People today, as never before, are realizing that He who is The Way is a necessity, thus the amazing religious revival that we now are experiencing.

Second, roads draw us closer together. There was a time when we were widely separated when we were only fifty miles apart. Now we think nothing of driving fifty miles just to have dinner with some friends. Roads make that difference.

One of the things I hate more than almost anything is prejudice. I have contempt for any person who thinks he is better than some other person. Our nation has suffered at the hands of the sowers of discord and division.

There will come a time when racial strife, bitter conflicts between capital and labor, denominational narrowness, and all the other things that separate us will disappear because, "In Christ there is no East or West, in Him no South or North; but one great fellowship of love throughout the whole wide earth."

Christ teaches us how to understand and love each other, how to be patient and how to forgive, how to "suffer long and be kind."

Third, roads make traveling so much easier and more pleasant. My back hurts now when I think of how we used to have to push the car when we were stuck on some muddy road. Now much of my work as a minister is trying to help people who are stuck on the way of life.

I talk to many people who believe they can break the moral laws and thereby live a happier and freer life. Again and again I have had people say that they wanted to get back on "the right way."

Of course, any road can be traveled in fair weather. But we get stuck when the rains come. Sooner or later, sorrows, disappointments, and all kinds of upsetting experiences may come. I have yet to see one person who could not go on if he were on "The Way."

Finally, roads carry us to places. It is very helpful for one to stop for a period of serious thinking about where he is going. There are a lot of people moving at a rather rapid rate up some blind alley. And since life is a one-way street and no one can turn around and come back, those people end up in frustration and defeat.

Not only does the right way lead us to a successful, free and happy life on this earth, it takes us into the life beyond. "Without Christ, death is a blind alley to oblivion. But with Christ, death is an open road to the Father's house."

Thomas said, "Lord, how can we know the way?" And many have felt that same thing. We are confused as to what really is the way of life. Jesus said, "I am the way." As we study Him, and commit our lives to the principles we learn from Him, we know we are on "The Way."

52. Forget It!

ONE OF THE greatest steps to a happy life is to learn how to forget. I have talked to a number of people who have had nervous break-downs. For the most part, they "broke down" because they were trying to carry too heavy a load. And in the majority of cases, that load was an accumulation of past mistakes and failures.

Had these people followed St. Paul's example, "Forgetting those things that are behind and reaching forth unto those things which are before, I press toward the mark." (Philippians 3:13, 14) they would have been able to go on living good and enjoyable lives. All people make mistakes. But successful people are those who have learned to forget *and go ahead.*

Right at this point is the cause of the break-down of a lot of homes. Here is a story that illustrates. A man met an old college friend downtown one night. They sat down in the lobby of the hotel and began to talk over old times. Before they realized it, it was long past midnight.

They went on home, but both of them were a little fearful of what their wives would say about their coming in so late. The next day they met again. One asked, "How did your wife take your coming in so late?" "Oh," the other replied, "I explained it to her and it was all right. What about your wife?"

"Well," he said, "when I came in my wife got historical."

153

"You mean 'hysterical,' don't you?" his friend asked.

"No," he said, "I mean 'historical.' She brought up everything that has happened the past thirty years."

I was blessed with a very wise father and he had some wonderful rules that he went by. There were seven of us children and there were times when things came up that were unpleasant. But one of his rules was that whatever came between one of us and him, he would settle it that night before we went to bed and never mention it again. He knew how to forget.

A lot of couples come to me to get married; often one and sometimes both have been divorced. Now I am opposed to divorces and I spend a lot of my time trying to prevent them from happening. Divorce is failure. But no failure needs be final.

So I usually talk to them about the fact that they can still have a happy marriage and home if they are willing to apply themselves, to be loving and kind and to work at it. But above all things, they must be willing to "forget those things that are behind." If they drag their past failures into their next marriage, it too will likely fail.

George Herbert said that when a person undresses for sleep at night, he should also undress his soul from the mistakes and failures of the day. One of the best ways to do that is to follow the advice of Jesus when he said: "Whosoever shall not receive the kingdom of God as a little child, he shall not enter therein" (Mark 10:15).

All of us remember how, as children, we would fall down and get a bruise. We would come crying to mother, who would take us in her arms and kiss the bruised place. Magically the pain would go away.

And it is wonderful to have that child-like faith that enables us to come to the loving Heavenly Father, simply confess our sins and hurts, to have Him remove the pain and let us start over again. A lot of people are too big and important to have such a simple faith, but I hope I never outgrow it.

Charles Wesley was inspired to write: "He breaks the power of cancelled sin, He sets the prisoner free." Of course, God is at all times ready to forgive but we must also do our part in the cancelling of our past sins and mistakes.

If you are carrying some burden of the past that you have not forgotten, first, ask yourself if there is anything you can do now to correct it, and make restitution. Do what you should and can, and then realize it is settled. If there is nothing you can do about it, then think of it no more. Forget and go ahead.

53. Life Is Good

"I COMPLAINED BECAUSE I had no shoes until I met a man who had no feet." A friend of mine used to have that saying hanging on the wall above his desk and he would read it to every person who came in his office complaining. He quoted it frequently.

It was easy for him, because he was truly on top. He had a beautiful office overlooking the city, and a large income. He had a fine home in one of the best residential sections and a lovely family. But a series of business reverses left him destitute. He was forced to move out of his beautiful office and out of his fine home. He and his wife now live in rented rooms.

He phoned that he wanted to come by and see me; I

knew of his reverses and I really dreaded his coming. I was sure he would be humiliated and broken and I was shocked when he walked in. He stood as straight as ever; he was smiling and he looked well. With a sigh of relief I told him to sit down and tell me about things.

He said, "I've still got my same old motto—'I complained because I had no shoes until I met a man who had no feet.' I've got a job and everything is good." I asked what he was doing and he named a job that an eighteen-year old boy could have handled. He is now making $200.00 a month. "Not much," he said, "but enough to pay the rent and buy groceries for my wife and me." And he added with a smile, "Provided we don't eat too much."

I told him that he was one of the greatest men I have ever known, and I wanted to know how he did it. I asked him his secret. This is what he told me: "I learned a long time ago that no matter what happens, life is good." So, instead of thinking about what he has lost, he is ever thinking about the good things in life that are ahead and it has made him a very happy man.

I am interested in a study made of a group of office workers. Though they all do practically the same work, at the close of the day some of them are gay and happy while others are limp with fatigue. The difference between the two groups is that the happy ones have something to look forward to.

I grew up in a series of small towns, and whenever I see friends from those towns I am asked, "How do you like Atlanta?" It takes me a while to answer that. I miss the smaller towns where you know everybody. A big city is the loneliest place in the world, and I must admit that I often feel a homesickness for the old home town.

On the other hand, to be the pastor of a church on the main thoroughfare of a great city is a challenging and thrilling opportunity. Something different happens every day. You become acquainted with all types of people. There is always much to do and, because I love my work, life for me is a great adventure. I know that life is good. But, there come into life those bitter and hard experiences—sorrows, hardships, disappointments. There are problems to which we can see no solution. And often, "when life tumbles in," it is hard to know that life is good.

"We know that all things work together for good to them that love God," said St. Paul (Romans 8:28). It is difficult to say that to a mother whose baby has just died, or to a man who has lost his job and is worrying about how to support his family, or to a girl whose boy-friend has jilted her, and to so many others.

But think of a ship. Not all parts of the ship will float by themselves,—for example, the propeller or the engine. But when all of the parts are built together they *do* float So in life. Not everything that happens is good. But when all of the experiences of life are taken as a whole and ce mented together by our love for God and His love for us, then we do know that no matter what happens, life is good and there is a lot to live for.